"J. T. Rogers combines the curious nature of a journalist with the erudition of a great playwright. Riveting and sprinkled with moments of great levity, the play yields details about the Oslo peace process that have never been disclosed in news articles or books or documentaries. It is edifying and entertaining, and it is an immensely valuable public service."

—RAJIV CHANDRASEKARAN, AUTHOR OF
IMPERIAL LIFE IN THE EMERALD CITY: INSIDE IRAQ'S GREEN ZONE

"Little about history is scripted. People and ideas matter. *Oslo* captures what happened in the Middle East when committed people and creative ideas came together—and, in the end, what did not happen when inertia and violence intervened. Blessed—and frustrated—are the peacemakers in this informative, true-to-life, and above all gripping play."

—RICHARD N. HAASS, PRESIDENT, COUNCIL ON FOREIGN RELATIONS

"An absorbing drama . . . A streamlined time machine . . . Rogers has done a fine job of mapping the lively, confusing intersection where private personalities cross with public roles. The relationships that emerge from within and between the opposing camps are steeped in a poignant multifacetedness, as sworn enemies find themselves tentatively speaking the language of friendship. Their understanding and re-creation of the signature styles of allies and enemies make for unexpected moments of personal catharsis and illumination."

—*NEW YORK TIMES*

"*Oslo* makes a complex historical event feel understandable, intimate and profoundly affecting. Darkly humorous comments permeate the tense conversations, arguments, impossible rifts, and grudging compromises that play out in swiftly paced scenes."

—ASSOCIATED PRESS

"With *Oslo*, J. T. Rogers (who has made a specialty out of distilling politically fraught global conflict situations into briskly compelling, lucid stage narratives), has created a play alive with tension, intrigue, humor, bristling intelligence, and emotional peaks that are subdued yet intensely moving . . . a play that concludes unexpectedly on a poignant note of hope . . . Rogers's drama artfully locates the human story in a delicate account of political diplomacy. This is a richly insightful play about culturally diverse people—Norwegians, Israelis, Palestinians—discovering deep-rooted shared desires and personal affinities."

—HOLLYWOOD REPORTER

"Despite our knowing the outcome at the outset, *Oslo* barrels forward with the tension and suspense of an edge-of-your-seat thriller. Then, in the final moments of a story, which could be experienced as one of illusory success tumbling into failure, Rogers delivers an almost unbearably moving message of authentic, unsentimental optimism which feels like a gift. An extraordinary play."

— JOHN WEIDMAN, TONY AWARD–WINNING LIBRETTIST OF
PACIFIC OVERTURES, ASSASSINS, AND CONTACT

"One of the year's best plays."   —*NJ STAR-LEDGER*

"*Oslo* gives you a fly-on-the-wall peek into one of the historic negotiations between the Israelis and Palestinians. It is gripping, provocative, wrenching, funny and altogether riveting. In *Oslo*, J. T. Rogers shows the insane amount of wrangling and linguistic gymnastics involved in enacting real political change. In place of soaring speeches, we get secret walks and after-hours drinking sessions that blur the line between enemy and friend and, more importantly, begin to shed the cloak of hatred that has obscured the humanity on both sides."

—HUFFINGTON POST

"Once there was a time when peace in the Middle East was tantalizing close. This is the stuff of the secret history of the region and a terrific new drama by J. T. Rogers. *Oslo* captures the willful ambiguities of the contentious Palestinian/Israeli relationship. Dramatic characters who in real-life crossed a forbidden political divide, then bonded as human beings despite personal risk. An improbable Norwegian couple brings these odd couples together. The rest is history. Part political thriller, part real-life drama. If you can't watch it, read it, there are revelations in both."

—DEBORAH AMOS, MIDDLE EAST CORRESPONDENT, NPR

"J. T. Rogers's *Oslo* manages a seemingly impossible feat: It transforms three hours of talk about the Oslo Accords into a gripping and urgent entertainment."

—*NJ.COM*

"The meticulous work behind the short-lived Accord leaves us even more hopeless about the world, but a bit more upbeat about the storytelling possibilities of the theater."

—*NEWSDAY*

"A cunning observation on the intricacies and absurdities of both international diplomacy and human relationships, *Oslo* wonderfully illustrates the importance of finding common ground and discovering one another's shared humanity. With a keen eye for cultural quirks and idiosyncrasies, J. T. Rogers is at his most funny and insightful when exploring the intersection between his characters' private and public persona."

— TINA BROWN, FOUNDER OF THE *DAILY BEAST* AND WOMEN IN THE WORLD

"Can we make peace with our enemies? Oslo gives us hope."

—*NY DAILY NEWS*

OSLO

OSLO

J. T. Rogers

THEATRE COMMUNICATIONS GROUP
NEW YORK
2017

The introduction, a version of the essay *"Oslo* and the Drama in Diplomacy" appeared in the *New York Times* on June 17, 2016.

The publication of *Oslo* by J. T. Rogers, through TCG's Book Program, is
made possible in part by the New York State Council on the Arts with the
support of Governor Andrew Cuomo and the New York State Legislature.

TCG books are exclusively distributed to the book trade by Consortium
Book Sales and Distribution.

Library of Congress Control Numbers:
2017004920 (print) / 2017004897 (ebook)
ISBN 978-1-55936-556-7 (trade paper) / ISBN 978-1-55936-876-6 (ebook)
A catalog record for this book is available from the Library of Congress.

Book design and composition by Lisa Govan
Art design by SpotCo

First Edition, April 2017
Third Printing, August 2017

For Bartlett Sher and André Bishop

CONTENTS

FOREWORD

Oslo was commissioned by Lincoln Center Theater, and it is a play that originated in a way that I wish more plays did, which is to say that it did not simply arrive by mail or email, and it did not appear on my desk as a hundred or so typed pages. It was a project that was developed with us from scratch.

One of the few genuinely political American playwrights working today, J. T. Rogers has cultivated a close partnership with LCT Resident Director Bartlett Sher, beginning when they collaborated on *Blood and Gifts*, produced with much success during our 2011–2012 season. For their collaboration on *Oslo*, J. T. spent more than two years reading documents of the negotiations, visiting Norway, and interviewing participants in the peace talks—world leaders, secret service agents, diplomats—traveling all over Europe, the US, and the Middle East. After synthesizing all that he had learned, he made an imaginative leap by asking the question all writers do: What if? What if these disparate characters were put together in the same room?

J. T. proceeded by skillfully assembling all the stories he had collected and corroborated, and then channeled his creative powers to provide answers to those "what ifs," by writing his own original work. *Oslo* is not a documentary. Obviously, the people portrayed in the play have real-life counterparts, but the characters in *Oslo*, and the words they speak, are entirely the playwright's. The author has described his play as "a scrupulously researched, meticulously written fiction."

Oslo profiles a group of colorful, intelligent men and women who come together under extremely fraught circumstances to try to achieve something that had never been attained before: a framework for an agreement between Israelis and Palestinians. The play is often very funny and often very moving: *Oslo*'s aim is to show that the attempt to negotiate a peaceful coexistence between two mortal enemies is a painstaking yet noble pursuit. Despite the fact that the situation in the Middle East continues to be as volatile as ever, J. T. magnanimously ends his play on a note of infinite possibility for the future.

We who produce new plays on a regular basis know what it is like to have an up-and-down artistic life. Some plays are hard to put on, and yet turn out well. Others can be bliss in the rehearsal room and don't really work onstage. *Oslo* is rare: a play that was conceived for the right reason, written for the right reason, directed by the right person, and performed by a skillful, exuberantly gifted and trusting cast. Audiences who saw the play could intuit that onstage harmony, that sublime and beautiful collaboration between artists working at their peak. Let us not forget that the first run of the play occurred during the most vicious and grotesque presidential election process in American history. Audiences came to the theater looking for inspiration, for solace, for hope, and they found what they were looking for.

—André Bishop
Lincoln Center Theater, NY
January 2017

INTRODUCTION

In early 2012, as my play *Blood and Gifts* was finishing its run at Lincoln Center Theater, my director, Bartlett Sher, arranged for me to have a drink with a friend of his. Terje Rød-Larsen was then a United Nations special envoy, focused on Lebanon. The two men and their families had become friends through their daughters, who attended middle school together. Bart had invited his friend to rehearsals of *Blood and Gifts* to talk to the cast about his work as a diplomatic negotiator in the Middle East. "I've asked him to meet with you," Bart told me. "Ask him questions about everything he's done. You'll find it fascinating."

Late on a bitterly cold January night, we met for warm drinks at an Upper West Side haunt a few blocks from the theater. Mr. Larsen had just seen my play. He was vivacious and charming, draped in understated European finery—including dress shoes so elegant I filed the detail away under the mental heading "Interesting Character Trait." Peppering him with questions, I learned that his wife, Mona Juul, was Ambassador, Deputy Permanent Representative of the Norway Mission to the UN. Further, that they had both been deeply involved for years in the politics of the Middle East.

"Twenty years ago, Mona and I were part of a historic event," Mr. Larsen said. As we ordered our second round, I asked him to tell me more.

As a playwright, I look to tell stories that are framed against great political rupture. I am obsessed with putting characters onstage who struggle with, and against, cascading world events—and who are changed forever through that struggle. While journalism sharpens our minds, the theater can expand our sense of what it means to be human. It is where we can come together in a communal space to hear ideas that grip us, surprise us—even infuriate us—as we learn of things we didn't know. For me, that is a deeply, thrillingly, political act. I hunt perpetually for these kinds of stories. I look for them everywhere, but sometimes the story finds you.

In that restaurant, Mr. Larsen explained that he and his wife were intimately involved with the making of the Oslo Accords. I knew of the first-ever peace deal between the State of Israel and the Palestine Liberation Organization. I'll never forget watching the signing ceremony in the White House Rose Garden on television, on September 13, 1993, seeing President Clinton preside over that historic handshake between the bitterest of enemies, Yitzhak Rabin, the Prime Minister of Israel, and Yasser Arafat, the Chairman of the Palestine Liberation Organization. I already knew the joy and the rage that handshake caused around the world.

Then he told me something I did not know: that there was a clandestine diplomatic back channel that had made the Accords possible. That without a handful of men and women—Israeli, Palestinian, and Norwegian—working in secret to try to alter the political reality of two peoples, those Accords never would have happened. And when I heard that, I knew the writing of my next play had begun.

I contacted Ms. Juul and asked if we could meet. She was surprised at my interest in these events, but eventually agreed to talk to me. In person she was charming as well, but far more reserved than her husband. She deftly steered the conversation away from her own career and achievements, graciously but firmly keeping herself from being the center of attention. "Yes, we were part of this back channel," she confirmed. "But the story is not us. The story is about those in that channel who risked their lives to try and change the world."

I began a years-long process of reading, travel, and interviews with multiple participants as I sought to understand the full history of the secret channel—what came to be known as the Oslo Channel—through which the Accords were birthed. Everything that Mr. Larsen and Ms. Juul had told me turned out to be in the public record—but they had downplayed their own involvement. Throughout our conversations they had focused on the accomplishments of the Israelis and Palestinians who were involved, but Mr. Larsen and Ms. Juul were the ones who midwifed the entire process. And, like the agreements themselves, their involvement proved to be deeply controversial. There are those who saw the Oslo Channel as a necessary and bold attempt to bring peace to the Middle East; there are others who saw it as reckless, naive meddling that only added to the anguish in this region.

The further I dug, the more gripped I became as a dramatist. Here was the stuff of theater—events that were almost preposterous in their strangeness: clandestine meetings, often run by those who had no experience with such things; people's lives constantly put at risk; governments threatened with calamity; emotions rising and falling at an operatic scale; people pushed to the brink of what they thought possible as friendships were fused and torn apart.

It became clear that Mr. Larsen and Ms. Juul would be characters at the very heart of the play. These were the sort of protagonists a writer looks for: two complicated, articulate people driven to achieve something far greater than themselves—people who stumble, make mistakes, but keep pushing on. As I researched,

I drew a tight bracket around the historic events directly preceding and occurring during the time of the Channel's existence. I burrowed into this sliver of history as deeply as I could, in order to summon a specific moment in time and place. Then I took the who, what, when, and where of journalism and threw them into a blender. I wanted to write a play, not a textbook or a reenactment. I sought to capture the *spirit* of those real events—their craziness, fear, joy, and heartbreak. I wanted to tell a story about men and women risking their own lives and challenging their own beliefs as they struggle without a road map toward peace.

The historic events in *Oslo* are all true, but I have taken dramatic liberties. I have theatricalized and reinvented—all to focus my play on the radical act at the center of the actual Oslo Channel.

In the middle of endless bloodshed and hatred, members of the Israeli Government and the PLO chose to sit across from their enemies and see them as human beings. Each side listened to the other and was permanently changed by that listening. I am awed by the personal and political courage that took. It is a moment of history that I do not want forgotten.

— J. T. Rogers
Hastings-on-Hudson, NY
January 2017

OSLO

PRODUCTION HISTORY

Oslo was commissioned and given its world premiere in New York City by Lincoln Center Theater (André Bishop, Producing Artistic Director; Adam Siegel, Managing Director; Hattie K. Jutagir, Executive Director of Development and Planning). Performances began June 16, 2016, in the Mitzi E. Newhouse Theater. The production then transferred to Broadway at the Vivian Beaumont Theater, beginning performances on March 23, 2017. The director was Bartlett Sher; the sets were designed by Michael Yeargan, the costumes were designed by Catherine Zuber, the lighting was designed by Donald Holder, the sound was designed by Peter John Still, the projections were designed by 59 Productions; the stage manager was Cambra Overend. Throughout, the cast was as follows:

JOHAN JORGEN HOLST	T. Ryder Smith
JAN EGELAND	Daniel Jenkins
MONA JUUL	Jennifer Ehle
TERJE RØD-LARSEN	Jefferson Mays
MARIANNE HEIBERG	Henny Russell
TORIL GRANDAL	Henny Russell
FINN GRANDAL	T. Ryder Smith
THOR BJORNEVOG	Christopher McHale
TROND GUNDERSEN	Jeb Kreager
AHMED QURIE	Anthony Azizi
HASSAN ASFOUR	Dariush Kashani
SHIMON PERES	Daniel Oreskes

YOSSI BEILIN	Adam Dannheisser
URI SAVIR	Michael Aronov
JOEL SINGER	Joseph Siravo
YAIR HIRSCHFELD	Daniel Oreskes
RON PUNDAK	Daniel Jenkins
AMERICAN DIPLOMAT	Christopher McHale
GERMAN HUSBAND	Jeb Kreager
GERMAN WIFE	Angela Pierce
SWEDISH HOSTESS	Henny Russell

Other parts were played by members of the company.

CHARACTERS

The Norwegians

JOHAN JORGEN HOLST	Foreign Minister; married to Marianne Heiberg
JAN EGELAND	Deputy Foreign Minister
MONA JUUL	Official in the Foreign Ministry; reports to Jan Egeland; married to Terje Larsen
TERJE RØD-LARSEN	Director of the Fafo Institute for Applied Social Sciences; married to Mona Juul
MARIANNE HEIBERG	Executive with the Fafo Institute; works for Terje Larsen; married to Johan Jorgen Holst
TORIL GRANDAL	Housekeeper and cook at the Borregaard Estate outside Oslo; married to Finn
FINN GRANDAL	Groundsman at the Borregaard Estate outside Oslo; married to Toril
THOR BJORNEVOG	Senior officer with the Police Intelligence Service
TROND GUNDERSEN	Officer with the Police Intelligence Service

The Palestinians

AHMED QURIE   Finance Minister for the Palestine
(also known as "Abu Ala")   Liberation Organization
HASSAN ASFOUR   Official PLO liaison with the
                             Palestinian Delegation at
                             multilateral US-sponsored talks

The Israelis

SHIMON PERES   Foreign Minister
YOSSI BEILIN   Deputy Foreign Minister
URI SAVIR   Director-General of the Foreign
                             Ministry
JOEL SINGER   Legal advisor to the Foreign
                             Ministry; senior law partner for a
                             Washington, DC, firm
YAIR HIRSCHFELD   Senior Professor of Economics at
                             the University of Haifa
RON PUNDAK   Junior Professor of Economics at
                             the University of Haifa

Supporting Roles (played by members of the company)

AMERICAN DIPLOMAT
PALESTINIAN DIPLOMAT
ISRAELI DIPLOMAT
OTHER DIPLOMATS
DELEGATES
JOURNALISTS
PALESTINIAN CITIZENS
ISRAELI CITIZENS
WAITERS
AIRPORT PASSENGERS
GERMAN HUSBAND
GERMAN WIFE
SWEDISH HOSTESS

TIME AND PLACE

April 1992 to September 1993.

Oslo, Norway, and other locations around the world.

NOTES

The use of a slash (/) marks the point of overlapping dialogue.

Paragraph breaks mid-speech show where one thought ends and another commences.

Pronunciation should be culturally precise. Throughout, characters pronounce names and places from other countries as those *from* those other countries do. For example, the Norwegians, Israelis, and Palestinians all pronounce Terje Larsen's first name as "TIE-yuh." The one exception to this rule is a specific character who badly mispronounces Larsen's first name. The only two instances of mispronunciation are noted in the script.

Each act gallops along as one long, unbroken scene—with time and place constantly shifting, events swiveling between cacophony and stillness, and characters slipping back and forth between speaking to each other and to us. Thus in presentation, eschew the lumbering naturalism of "realistic" staging and design. Best to make choices that allow for lightness, rapidity, and theatrical surprise.

Out of the crooked timber of humanity,
no straight thing was ever made.

—Immanuel Kant

ACT ONE

Oslo, Norway. March 1993. Evening.

An elegant flat, mid-dinner. Laughter and champagne. Terje Rød-Larsen, forties, mid-story to his guests: Johan Jorgen Holst, fifties, and his wife, Marianne Heiberg, forties.

LARSEN: It's all true. I'm not making this up.

I'm sitting there in his office, in Tel Aviv, straight across from him, and before either of us even speak, I realize: it's not even noon, and he's drunk.

MARIANNE: No!

HOLST: He's exaggerating. Terje *always* embellishes.

LARSEN: Johan Jorgen, his words were completely slurred. I could *smell* the scotch on his breath!

MARIANNE: Are you saying that Yitzhak Rabin is an alcoholic?

LARSEN: Not at all. Just that he drinks. Heavily.

(Seamlessly back to it) I start to introduce myself—and he cuts me off! Just launches in, about the Israeli Labor Party, as its Chairman; the upcoming elections; platitude, platitude; and *then* he says:

11

(As Rabin, in a gravelly voice) "Mr. Larsen, as a French politician, you will understand what I am saying."

(As himself again) "Excuse me." I am polite, but firm. "I am a Norwegian and I am not a politician."

HOLST: Not by a long shot.

MARIANNE: Johan Jorgen, let him talk.

LARSEN: And he goes on, as if I've said nothing. And once again:

(As Rabin) "As a Frenchman, you will—"

And I completely break protocol.

(Himself, to Rabin) "Listen! I am Norwegian, I run the Fafo Institute *in* Norway, and I want that to be clear!"

The meeting ends, I leave, and I think to myself: What the fuck is this guy doing running the Israeli Labor Party?

(As Mona Juul, thirties, enters with a fresh bottle of champagne . . .)

MARIANNE: Mona, can you believe Terje said that to Yitzhak Rabin?

MONA: My husband shows no deference to power.

LARSEN: Well, what is a throne but a stool covered in velvet?

MONA: You've used that one before.

LARSEN: Have I?

MARIANNE: Yes, / you have. Repeatedly.

HOLST: Many, many / times. Over and over.

LARSEN: The *point* of this story is this: six months later, Rabin is Prime Minister and I am a fool. Why? Because I saw one side of this man and assumed this meant I knew all of him. Now I tell you all this, not to speak of myself—

HOLST: Well, this *is* an occasion.

LARSEN: But to speak of you, Johan Jorgen.

Had *you* been there, *you* would have seen to the very core of this man. For like Rabin himself, you are a visionary and bold statesman: able to see what others cannot; willing to act when others will not.

Tomorrow you are Foreign Minister, and all of us in this country will be better off under your stewardship.

(Raising his glass) To Johan Jorgen Holst. May your eyes be open to the new as you steer our ship toward uncharted shores.

(They toast. Mona turns to us.)

MONA: To clarify: Johan Jorgen is married to Marianne, who works for Terje, who is married to me, who, as of tomorrow, works for Johan Jorgen. In Norway we take nepotism to an entirely new level. It's a very small country and we think and behave as such.

(She is back with them. Larsen has ceded the floor to Holst.)

HOLST: I'll tell you what I'm *not* looking forward to: dealing with Warren Christopher.
Mona, have you met him?

MONA: Not yet.

HOLST: My God, what a wet fish. *This* is the new US Secretary of State? No wonder the Americans can't make peace in the Middle East.

LARSEN: Then why don't you?

HOLST: What, make peace in the Middle East?

LARSEN: Why not?

MARIANNE: Because it's the Middle East, Terje. They don't *do* peace.

LARSEN: Ah, but my friends, look at what is happening in the world: the grip of history is loosening. The Berlin Wall has just fallen; the Soviet Empire, disbanded. My God, if Leningrad can revert to St. Petersburg, anything is possible.

MARIANNE: Terje, if the Americans can't force the Israelis and Palestinians to make a deal, what chance has Johan Jorgen?

LARSEN: But that's their problem. The Americans can strong-arm both parties to the table, but just because you drag a horse into a bar does not mean it can mix its own cocktail.

(Holst and Marianne gesture to Mona: "What?"
Mona gestures in response: "Don't ask.")

We have what the US can never have: the appearance of neutrality. The Americans flood Israel with foreign aid.
(Cutting Marianne off before she can speak) Which, as you know, I support one thousand percent.
(Back to Holst) But the perception is bias.

HOLST: So now I should take advice from a sociologist.

(To Marianne) Is this what you two are doing at your think tank? Sitting in your offices, funded by *my* ministry, is this what you're all saying?

LARSEN: It is what *I* am saying, Johan Jorgen. *Me.*

MONA: Terje does have a point.

(Holst and Marianne look at her in surprise.)

We *are* trusted by both sides. We have always supported Israel *and* the Palestinian cause, / while maintaining a strict neutrality on the issue of statehood.

HOLST: Mona! The Palestinian cause is led by Arafat and the PLO, who wish to wipe Israel off the map. Are you seriously suggesting Rabin talk peace with the man the Israelis call Hitler in his lair?

LARSEN: Johan Jorgen, you don't make peace with the people you have dinner parties with. You make peace with the people who bomb your markets and blow up your buses.

MARIANNE: Please, let's not talk politics. / It's Johan Jorgen's last night as a free man.

HOLST *(Straight at Larsen)*: While dinner was superb, / I cannot say the same thing for your ideas. You seem not to realize, Terje, that the job of the Foreign Minister is not to joust with windmills.

LARSEN *(Straight at Holst)*: What are you afraid of, Johan Jorgen? The world is cracking open. All I am saying is to think about new possibilities. Imagine what can be achieved *now!*

(A phone rings. Larsen and Mona freeze.
The two of them gesture to each other: "They're early!" "What do we do?"
Holst and Marianne watch in confusion as a second phone starts to ring.
Larsen answers the first phone just as Mona answers the second.)

LARSEN: This is Larsen.   MONA: Good evening.

(First phone to his ear, Larsen looks to Mona; second phone to her ear, she nods.)

LARSEN *(Into first phone)*: Yes, Those Across The Sea are with us. Now, to pick up where we last—

(Mona holds the second phone away from her and whispers in Larsen's ear.)

(Into the first phone) . . . Just one—hold on, please.

(Larsen switches phones with Mona. He listens to someone on the second phone. Then they switch back. Speaking into the first phone again:)

Those Across the Sea have a message they wish the Son to pass on to the Father.

HOLST: Terje, who are you talking to?

(Terje and Mona gesture silently and wildly: "For God's sake, be quiet!")

LARSEN *(Into the first phone again)*: They say they have waited long enough and they must know if the Grandfather is on board.

(He listens to the voice on the other end. It finishes. He gestures for Mona to give him the second phone. He holds both phones now.)

(Into the second phone) The Son wishes me to inform you that it is too early to say the ways of his Grandfather.

(The voice on the line starts screaming. We can't hear the words, but the rage is volcanic. Larsen throws that phone to Mona, who muffles the shouting with her hand.)

(Back into the first phone) They say that's fine, no problem, talk soon.

(Larsen and Mona hang up their phones as one.)

HOLST: What the hell was that?

LARSEN: My apologies. I had the time zones wrong, clearly. I thought they were calling much later.

HOLST: Terje. Who were you talking to?

LARSEN *(Raising the first phone)*: The Israeli Government . . . *(Pointing at the second phone)* . . . and the PLO.

(Holst and Marianne burst into laughter. Then they stop laughing. They realize that Larsen is serious.)

I was going to tell you before they called. I'm truly sorry.

HOLST: What is this?

What the hell is going on?

LARSEN: I am facilitating secret conversations between the State of Israel and the Palestine Liberation Organization. They are meeting, here in Norway, face-to-face, not far from here.

(Silence. Then, cacophony.)

HOLST: Are you mad? / Have you gone completely mad?

MARIANNE: Terje! How could you not tell me?

HOLST: You have / absolutely no authority to do this!

LARSEN: Please, my friends, please!

MARIANNE: I am your partner!

LARSEN: I think *associate* is the / official title, yes?

MARIANNE: You would risk our entire organization / like this without my involvement?

LARSEN: Actually, *my* organization. That *I* founded.

HOLST: Who approved this?!

MONA: I did.

(Holst freezes.)

Paperwork, visas. I arranged everything.

We are in this together.

(He stares at her. She stares back.)

HOLST: Who else in the Ministry knows about this?

MONA: Egeland does.

(Turning to us) Jan Egeland, Deputy Foreign Minister, who I report to, and who, when we were at university . . . it was complicated.

Again, it's a very small country.

(Holst paces; the others watch.)

HOLST: So. The night before I take office: *this* is when you deign to tell me there is a ticking bomb *in* my office.

How high up does this go in Israel?

MONA: We're not sure.

HOLST: But Shimon Peres *is* behind this, yes?

MONA: We can't say.

MARIANNE: Well then what do the Americans say?

(Larsen and Mona look at each other. Then . . .)

MONA: They don't. Know much about it.

(Silence. Then:)

HOLST: Fuck / fuck fuck fuck fuck fuck fuck FUCK!

LARSEN: Johan Jorgen, it's fine—everything is going to be fine.

HOLST: I forbid this! Do you understand me? / Categorically!

LARSEN: Johan Jorgen—

HOLST: You are a fucking dilettante!

(To Mona) You work for me!

(To them both) And this is over!

A shift.

Terje speaks outward, addressing a packed lecture hall; Mona speaks to us.

LARSEN: In International Relations, most conflicts are negotiated using the model of Totalism. All issues of disagreement are placed on the table; all organizations, representing all sides, are *at* the table. The rules are rigid, the procedure impersonal, and time and again the results are absolute failure. Thus to facilitate an *effective* negotiation, you must learn to use the model of Gradualism.

MONA: When I was at university, Terje's lectures on organizational psychology were always packed.

LARSEN: This new model—*my* model—is rooted not in the organizational but in the personal. A process of negotiation allowing the most implacable of adversaries to focus on a single issue of contention; resolve it, then move on to the *next* single issue; as they gradually build a bond of trust.

MONA: He was my teacher, I was his student. I argued with him, he argued back. Drinks, marriage: the usual.

LARSEN: But hear me: to use this model is not without risk. For when you unleash the personal, the Furies can come out. And once this process begins, there is no going back. Events will move faster and faster, stretching you to the breaking point. But through it all, you must push on. Believing that whatever mistakes are made, whatever unforeseen events your actions unleash, the risks are worth it. Because if you succeed, you will change the world.

MONA: That is what I needed you to hear. Because this idea, this *process* is what drove everything—*everything*—we said and did. As you watch, and judge, remember that.

Bodies to and fro on the stage. Mona continues to speak to us.

MONA: Cairo. One year earlier. My first posting overseas. Terje came with me. We threw ourselves into the region, traveling everywhere. But one small country kept drawing us back.

LARSEN: Mona, my God!

MONA: Jerusalem, Tel Aviv.

LARSEN: I love this place!

MONA: The West Bank, Gaza.

LARSEN: I love these people! All of them—they're so fantastically *not* Norwegian!

MONA: Gaza was like nothing we had ever seen.

A mere strip of land, hugging the Mediterranean. Physically cut off from the West Bank by Israel itself.

The most densely populated place on earth.

LARSEN: Mona! No one has ever done a proper scientific survey of living conditions here. *I* can be the one to do this!

MONA: A million Palestinians, most of them without regular electricity or water, crammed into an area twenty-five-miles long and only a few miles wide. A population exploding, with no place *to* explode.

PALESTINIAN CITIZEN *(In Arabic)*: [Death to Israel!]

MONA: We were in a back alley there when we walked into it.

PALESTINIAN CITIZEN *(In Arabic)*: [Long live Arafat!]

MONA: A crowd, seething. Soldiers rushing.

PALESTINIAN CITIZEN *(In Arabic)*: [Long live Arafat!]

MONA: Terje and I crouched behind an upturned car as bodies fell. And then we saw it.

Two boys facing each other, one in uniform, one in jeans, weapons in hand, hate flowing between them. But their faces—and we both see this—their faces are exactly the same. The same fear. The same desperate desire to be anywhere but here. To *not* be doing this, *to* this other boy. And there, in that moment, for us, it began.

Later. Terje and Mona at the UN Club in the Gaza Strip.

MONA: Terje, be serious.

LARSEN: I am *beyond* serious.

MONA: The plan you are proposing is not possible.

LARSEN: No, it is not *probable*. But if there is even a *two*-percent chance, how can we not take it? Mona. What we just witnessed . . . would you not try anything to give those two boys a different narrative?

(He crosses to her. Hand to her face.)

Step back and look at the world, my love. The old order is falling away. The unthinkable is becoming thinkable. In our lifetime there will not be another moment like this. *This* is our chance to make a difference.

(They stare at each other.)

MONA: Fine. Go ahead and try.

LARSEN: No, no. We are partners, in all things. I cannot do this without you. After all, who am I? But you, my darling, you are Mona Juul, jewel of the Norwegian Foreign Service. Who possesses the most . . .
(Each word with a kiss) beautiful . . . powerful . . . Rolodex.
Let us try, my love. Together.

MONA *(To us)*: Tell me you would have said no.

Yossi Beilin, forties, appears and speaks outward to us.

BEILIN: It's a circus! Madness!

MONA *(To us)*: Yossi Beilin. Rising star of the Israeli Labor Party, right arm and protégé of the great Shimon Peres.

BEILIN: These multinational negotiations have gone on for *two years.*

MONA: Yes, Yossi, I know.

BEILIN: Madrid, Washington—

MONA AND BEILIN: Now London—

BEILIN: A hundred and sixty delegates, all saying one thing in the room, something else to the cameras, and something completely different to their own people!

MONA *(To us)*: One month later. A tandoori restaurant. Tel Aviv. Israel is days away from parliamentary elections. Beilin is running for office. But I push and he agrees to meet briefly with Terje.

Lunchtime. Beilin and Larsen at a table together. A waiter brings food.

LARSEN: What you are describing sounds like a farce.

BEILIN: It's more than a farce, it's bullshit!

Our government refuses to negotiate directly with the PLO, so they are not at the table. But, of course, every Palestinian *at* the table has been hand-picked *by* the PLO.

(As he vents on, we see Ahmed Qurie, fifties, in a dark suit, his visage grim.)

Every day, Ahmed Qurie, the PLO's Finance Minister, is in a hotel across from the negotiations, on the phone, telling the Palestinian delegation *exactly* what to say. Yesterday, the two sides spent twelve hours haggling over one word! I don't know whether to laugh or— AAAH!

(Beilin doubles over in pain.)

LARSEN: Are you all right?

BEILIN: Yes, I'm just— AAAH!
(Sitting up, unsteady) My apologies. Spicy food does not agree with me. Whenever I eat anything more adventurous than gefilte fish my body rebels.

LARSEN: You should have told me. We could have gone / somewhere else.

BEILIN: It's no use. I can't give up the idea that suddenly everything will change and my stomach will be my friend. So, you see, I am dreaming of two peace plans simultaneously. *(Shaking his head)* We are racing toward a precipice. The Intifada has been going on in Gaza for five years. The Palestinians are killing our settlers, and our soldiers, and themselves; our army is shooting back and children are getting killed; and it is all on CNN and it is a fucking disaster. In Europe they are calling us Nazis. In *Europe*. Where it has only been *fifty years*. Every day, more and more of the world turns against us, but all we do is sit at that fucking negotiating table—

LARSEN: Where you will achieve nothing because your negotiating model is fundamentally flawed.

BEILIN: Exactly! That's what *I* / keep saying!

LARSEN: You are trapped in a procedure that is rigid, impersonal, / and incapable of building trust.

BEILIN: Yes. Yes. I agree—completely!

But this is what the Americans want us to do.

LARSEN: And so you must do it.

But, also, establish a second channel, built on the exact opposite model. Not grand pronouncements between governments, but intimate discussions between people. Held somewhere isolated—totally—where you and the PLO can meet, alone, and talk.

This model, I can oversee; this place, I can arrange.

(Beilin stares at him.)

BEILIN: How?

LARSEN: The resources of my institute Fafo, my expertise: all at your disposal. Discretion guaranteed.

(Silence. Then:)

BEILIN *(Excited now)*: This . . . this could be amazing.

/ This could potentially unblock and get things moving.

LARSEN *(Equally so)*: I think so, yes. A tributary. To feed the main channel.

(Beilin has another fit.)

BEILIN *(Fighting through it)*: If we win the election, Shimon will be Foreign Minister and I will be his Deputy. It is illegal for any Israeli official to speak to the PLO. But. Someone *un*official.

LARSEN: Who you and Peres would choose.

BEILIN: That you could introduce to—

LARSEN: Exactly what I'm thinking, yes.

BEILIN: *If* we win.

MONA *(To us)*: They did.

A hotel suite in London. Mona is with Ahmed Qurie—as ever in a formal dark suit.

QURIE: My eldest daughter is named Mona. She is the light of my life. This bodes well for our meeting.

MONA: Thank you for making time to meet me, Mr. Qurie.

QURIE: Of course. Norway has always been a robust supporter of the Palestinian people. And I have heard greatly of you and have long wished to see you in the flesh. *(Beat)* Perhaps that is not the correct / use of this word.

MONA: No, it's fine. Understood. I'm so pleased our work brings us to London at the same time.

QURIE: Ah, well, *you* are here for work, but alas I am here for foolishness. *(Pointing)* In that hotel, across, they are negotiating for the future of Palestine. Yet I, who am the Finance Minister of the PLO, I am banned! Barred! Blocked from the very table where the economic future of my people is to be determined!

MONA: And I would like to talk to you about / that very situation.

QURIE *(On a roll now)*: Meanwhile, in Gaza, our children throw the very stones of their houses and are returned by the bullets of the occupying—

MONA: Mr. Qurie. You don't need to give me the speech.

QURIE: Of course. You are on our side.

MONA: And theirs.

QURIE: Ms. Juul. You have spent some time in my region and your intentions are no doubt cloaked in virtue, but perhaps there are still factors you do not understand.

MONA: Do you mean I don't understand that your Chairman Arafat's recent backing of Saddam Hussein in the Gulf War so infuriated your now-former Arab allies that they expelled ninety thousand Palestinian guest workers, thereby creating such a financial catastrophe for your people that now the PLO is stuck in Tunis, unable to pay even your electricity bills? Or do I not understand that without additional support from my government your organization will slide one step closer to irrelevancy?

(They stare at each other.)

QURIE: I see that you are, what is the phrase?, irritatingly well informed.

MONA: Tell me how much you need and I will do what I can. But I want you to do one thing.

QURIE: Of course. For you I will—

MONA: Not for me. For you.

There is a man being sent to London. For you to meet.

QURIE: Who is this man?

Beilin and Larsen speak out to us.

BEILIN: Terje, I've picked the man I'm sending.

(Yair Hirschfeld, forties, unkempt and sloppily dressed, appears.)

Yair Hirschfeld, Professor of Economics.

HIRSCHFELD *(To us)*: A rabbi and a Buddhist priest are on a plane. The rabbi turns to the Buddhist priest and says: "I will never forgive your people for Pearl Harbor."

The priest stares at him. "What are you talking about? I'm Chinese! I had nothing to do with that!"

The rabbi shrugs. "Chinese, Japanese, what's the difference?"

The priest leans in.

"I will never forgive *your* people for the Titanic." "The Titanic!" shouts the rabbi. "That was an iceberg!"

The priest shrugs: "Iceberg, Goldberg, what's the difference?"

LARSEN *(To Beilin)*: Really?

BEILIN: Trust me, he's the man for the job.

LARSEN: It's just, he's a bit, if I may say, déclassé.

BEILIN: Well, he's from Haifa.

A shift. Larsen and Mona alone.

MONA: Stay with Ahmed Qurie in his hotel suite. I'll be with Hirschfeld in a room nearby. When I give the signal, they will enter a third room.

Qurie appears, agitated. He speaks outward as Mona continues to speak to Larsen.

QURIE: I have set aside but a few minutes for this meeting.

MONA: Qurie is not to know what the conversation will be about—for his own safety.

Qurie's hotel suite; Larsen alone with the anxious PLO Minister. At the same time, Hirschfeld and Mona in another hotel room; the professor riven with anxiety.

QURIE: The minutes are ticking, Mr. Larsen. What is the delay?

HIRSCHFELD: Look at my hands. I can't make them stop.
Can I have some water?

MONA: Dr. Hirschfeld, I think you should go in.

LARSEN *(To Qurie)*: Please, you must relax. Everything will be fine.

HIRSCHFELD: It's one thing to think about doing this to, to—for years—but to actually—I *really* would like some water.

MONA: After. I promise. You *must* go in.

QURIE: If he extends his hand first I will not shake it. I am of ministerial rank. If there is a shaking of hands, I will initiate.

HIRSCHFELD: I am not here as my government. He knows this, right? It is against the law, Ms. Juul, for any Israeli official / to meet with the PLO.

MONA: Yes, yes, he knows.
Now, you know *exactly* what you are going to say, yes?

HIRSCHFELD: Yes.

LARSEN: Good, right; here we go.

(Qurie does not move.)

What's wrong?

QURIE *(A moment, then . . .)*: I have never met an Israeli. Face-to-face.

(As one, Hirschfeld and Qurie step forward. They are alone. Staring at each other.)

HIRSCHFELD: Hello.

QURIE: Hello.

(Neither moves.)

HIRSCHFELD: London is very cold this time of year.
QURIE: Yes.

(Stillness. Silence.)

HIRSCHFELD: And wet.
QURIE: Yes.
HIRSCHFELD: Not like home.
QURIE: I have not been home since 1967 when every man, woman, and child in my village was forced to flee our homeland before the advancing hordes of Zionism.
HIRSCHFELD: Ah.
QURIE *(Beat, then . . .)*: But I remember well the warmth there this time of year.
HIRSCHFELD: I read your latest paper.
QURIE *(Surprised)*: Ah.
HIRSCHFELD: I thought it excellent.
QURIE: Thank you.
HIRSCHFELD: Economic cooperation between our peoples: I could not agree more.
QURIE: Yes, it is the only way for us to move forward.
HIRSCHFELD: Because, God knows, the American-sponsored talks going on here in London are going nowhere.
QURIE *(Waving his hand)*: The dialogue of the deaf. Talk *at*, never *to*. / Never listening.
HIRSCHFELD: Yes, I agree. Completely.

I have written a paper of my own, demonstrating the benefits of such economic cooperation. Using a gravity model, I establish the possibility of substantial GDP growth / for both economies, resulting from the removal of trade barriers.
QURIE: Yes. Yes. Substantial GDP growth, for *both* sides. In my work, I have reached the same conclusion.
HIRSCHFELD: Perhaps if you could read it. Give me your professional feedback.
QURIE: I would be honored.

MONA *(To us)*: They spoke for two hours. I was forced to knock.

QURIE: This has been . . . fruitful.

HIRSCHFELD: I agree.

QURIE: You have been most generous with your thoughts.

HIRSCHFELD: We should meet again. To discuss. Economics. The future.
(Memorized) I'm told if we were to meet in Oslo, friends would prove . . . sorry . . . *(Correcting and reciting again)* . . . I'm told if we were to meet in Oslo, friends would *provide* us solitude and privacy and anything else we would require.

(They stare at each other.)

QURIE: Who are you?

HIRSCHFELD: I am just a professor of economics who supports dialogue with the PLO.

QURIE: But on whose authority do you speak?

HIRSCHFELD: I have no authority.

QURIE: Then you are not a man with whom I can / afford to meet again.

HIRSCHFELD: But I *am* having breakfast tomorrow morning in Tel Aviv with my dear, good friend Yossi Beilin. I am so looking forward to telling him about my trip to London.

QURIE: Yossi Beilin.

HIRSCHFELD: Yes.

QURIE: The new Israeli Deputy Foreign Minister.

HIRSCHFELD: Yes.

QURIE: You are saying Beilin speaks to *you*?

HIRSCHFELD: Where you and I come from, is that not what friends do?

The Larsen flat. Evening.
Larsen and Mona watch a shocked Jan Egeland, thirties, pace as he takes in the news.

EGELAND: My God! I mean, I mean—my God!

MONA *(To us)*: Once again, Jan Egeland, *our* Deputy Foreign Minister.

LARSEN: No one at my institute knows about this.

MONA: No one else in the Ministry.

Jan, if we set up a meeting, Ahmed Qurie will come as the voice of the PLO.

EGELAND: Mona! There *is* no voice of the PLO but Arafat's! Beneath him it's a labyrinth of backstabbing factions—and you know this!

(Cutting Mona off before she can speak) Who is this Ahmed Qurie? How can you be sure this man has even told Arafat what he is doing?

MONA: Because Terje went to Tunis and spent the day with Arafat.

(Larsen holds up a photo and hands it to Egeland.)

LARSEN: A little commemoration.

EGELAND *(Eyes on the photo)*: My God!

MONA: I wanted to make sure Arafat was fully informed and behind it before I brought this to you.

LARSEN: For a bloodstained terrorist he's terribly charming.

(As Arafat) "Ah, Mr. Larsen! We must find a way to let a thousand flowers bloom."

(Himself again) Most of what he says makes no sense, but he says it with great panache.

MONA: The photo—Arafat and Terje—was so the Israelis, too, would know this is legitimate. If we host it, they're on board.

EGELAND: *Yossi Beilin* is on board, Mona, who does not have the authority to / authorize such a thing.

LARSEN: Jan. Jan. Yossi told me—to my face—this comes directly from Shimon Peres. The orchestrator of every diplomatic breakthrough the Israelis have ever achieved—*he* is behind this, absolutely.

(The three of them stare at each other.)

MONA: The Minister listens to you, Jan. He trusts you. All we need is his tacit approval.

LARSEN: We will say that my institute, Fafo, is bringing Israeli and Palestinian academics here to Norway for a conference. No one but us will know the truth.

MONA: No diplomatic channels. Regular flights, routes randomly chosen.

If you say no, this conversation never happened.

Isn't that right, Terje?

LARSEN: Of course. But I'm sure Jan sees the extraordinary—

MONA: Jan can see whatever he wishes.

(To Egeland) This is his call.

(Silence. Then . . .)

EGELAND: Let's fucking do it.

I'll get the Old Man to look the other way.

But we tell no one else. And this is not being done through the Ministry.

(To Larsen) Officially this is Fafo's scheme. If this goes to shit, it's all on you.

LARSEN: Understood.

EGELAND: A megalomaniac acting on his own.

LARSEN: That makes / complete sense.

EGELAND: A preening, narcissistic dilettante who / loves the sound of his own voice.

LARSEN: I think we're all clear now, thank you.

EGELAND: Good.

LARSEN: And don't tell the Americans.

MONA: Terje, what are you talking about? We can't not tell the Americans.

LARSEN: Tell them what? "Nothing has happened and we thought you should know that"?

MONA: The Americans view the Middle East as theirs. Do you know what their government will do to ours if we are caught meddling without permission?

LARSEN: Mona! How are things going to stay hidden if the Americans are involved? It will be over before it begins. / Look at their record with keeping secrets. Disastrous!

MONA: This is a diplomatic issue, Terje, which is not your concern.

EGELAND: I agree with Terje.

If we're going to take a risk, let's take a risk.

When I'm next in Washington, at the State Department, I'll make a casual mention of what we're doing. No details; slipped in among other remarks. They won't pay attention and our hands will be clean.

(They all look at each other.)

So.
Here we go.

Qurie appears. He and Larsen talk outward, as if on the phone.

QURIE: When we arrive you will meet us personally. No one will touch our passports but you.

(Beilin appears, speaking outward to Larsen as well.)

BEILIN: Israel is not involved in these discussions. Hirschfeld and his associate are speaking only for themselves.
QURIE: While we are there, we are not there.
BEILIN: Terje, you cannot even use the *word* "negotiations"—or "talks"—or I will pull the plug. Do you understand?
QURIE: Deniability, Mr. Larsen, in all matters.
BEILIN: If word gets out, Terje—
QURIE: If word gets out, Mr. Larsen—
BEILIN: My government will fall.
QURIE: I will be killed. Undoubtedly.
Here, to speak with the devil is to become the devil.
When I arrive, my life will be in your hands.

(Qurie is gone.)

BEILIN: Terje . . . Do you know what I fear most? That we will risk everything to sit across from them, only to find that there is nothing for us to discuss.

(Beilin is gone.)

MONA *(To us):* Terje made calls.

LARSEN: I can't give you details but I need to borrow your place, and its staff. They must be sworn to secrecy.

MONA *(To us):* Borregaard Castle, south of Oslo, far from anywhere.

LARSEN: I beg you, you must tell no one.

MONA *(To us):* He rented cars. We checked their flights. We rechecked their flights. And then, the night before, disaster.

The stage floods with diplomats and journalists, mikes and cameras in hand.

MONA *(To us):* An Israeli border guard is murdered and his body mutilated by Palestinians. In retaliation, four hundred Palestinians accused of terrorist links are deported to the freezing rocky ground of southern Lebanon. Where they are abandoned on a hilltop. Without blankets, food, or water.

PALESTINIAN DIPLOMAT: The blood of four hundred will be on the head of Yitzhak Rabin!

ISRAELI DIPLOMAT: Israel will meet peace with peace and violence with violence!

Mona and Larsen in their flat.

MONA: Call it off.

LARSEN: It's fine. / Everything is fine.

MONA: If you won't do it, I will. Men have been killed, Terje. People are rioting.

LARSEN: I know, it's tragic, but these are perfect conditions for progress. The desperation they are feeling, on both sides, *this* is our ally.

MONA: And when they turn that desperation on us?

LARSEN: Who knows! We will improvise as we go.

MONA: Terje! This is not something you make up as you go along! If this fails: Fafo, the Ministry—our lives—will all be / torn down!

LARSEN: Mona, you must trust me! More than you have ever done before. I know how to do this. I *see* how to do this.

(They stare at each other. Neither moves. Then:)

MONA: You yourself will play no direct role in these talks.

LARSEN: Of course not. Darling, I told you: my model is the opposite of the / American approach.

MONA: Whatever happens between them, we cannot interfere. Our behavior must be beyond reproach. If we are seen— by anyone—as meddling, as favoring / one side over the other.

LARSEN: Darling, I would never do such a thing.

MONA: Then say it.

You will facilitate, and facilitate only.

Say it.

LARSEN: I will facilitate. Only.

Reception room of Borregaard Estate, outside Sarpsborg, the next morning. Larsen stands in the middle of the well-appointed room. In front of him, Qurie and Hassan Asfour (forties), both in dark suits and ties, stand facing Hirschfeld and a grinning Ron Pundak (thirties), both more casually dressed.

MONA *(To us)*: January 1993. The official opening of the unofficial Oslo Channel. From here on, everything else that happened, everything you will see, took place in only nine months.

LARSEN: Some of us have met, of course, but let us have a proper introduction.

(Gesturing to them) From the Palestine Liberation Organization, Mr. Ahmed Qurie and his associate, Mr. Hassan Asfour . . .

(Gesturing to them) . . . And from the University of Haifa, Professor Yair Hirschfeld and Professor Ron Pundak.

PUNDAK *(To Qurie)*: Hello!

(To Asfour) Hello!

(To them all) Hello!

LARSEN: Gentlemen, this regal and historic guesthouse that we are standing in, it is the very site where eight hundred years ago, Saint Olaf himself erected his castle, stone by stone, as he strove to make Norway into a nation.

ASFOUR: And your Olaf was killed and his castle destroyed in a landslide.

LARSEN: Thank you. So appreciated.

PUNDAK *(Boundless cheer)*: I don't know about the rest of you but I have never *seen* so much snow. My God, it's cold here.

ASFOUR: Not as cold as the rocky ground of southern Lebanon. You should have killed those four hundred. *That* would have sent us a message. But instead, they shiver on that hilltop and their faces are on every television in the world, and you are condemned.

You do not believe in your cause enough to do what must be done. That is your weakness.

LARSEN: And, again, so appreciated.

(To the group) You are here because you know that your people cannot go on as you have. That whatever you personally feel, you wish to find a way forward. But to overcome hatred and fear, pragmatism is not enough.

Now, Abu Ala, tell us—

QURIE *(Taken aback)*: I am Ahmed Qurie.

LARSEN: But your friends call you Abu Ala, yes?

QURIE: Yes, but—

LARSEN: And here we are all friends.

While we are together, this will be our one unbreakable rule.

(Pointing to a shut door) In that room, when that door is closed, you will converse. Disagree. Worse. But out here we will share our meals, talk of our families, and light the fire.

(To them all) My friends, I must insist upon this rule. For it is only through the sharing of the *personal* that we can see each other for who we truly are.

(Larsen gestures to the closed door.
Silence.)

HIRSCHFELD: I—we—accept your rule.

(To Qurie and Asfour) And are willing to try.

ASFOUR *(To Qurie, in Arabic)*: [We should leave.]

QURIE *(To Asfour, in Arabic)*: [That is my decision.]

ASFOUR: [He is biased. He is not an honest broker. / This is a mistake. We need to fly home now.]

QURIE: [That's enough, we are here. We've come this far.]

(All look at Qurie. He looks back.)

Between our peoples lies a vast ocean. Upon it, great boats are but skiffs. Those before us have always turned back. Or drowned. Let us be the first to cross and step upon the other's shore.

(The four men turn to face the door.)

LARSEN: Good luck.

(As he starts to leave, all of them, in alarm:)

QURIE: Where are / you going?

HIRSCHFELD: / Are we not starting?

PUNDAK: We agreed to everything you asked.

LARSEN: It is your ocean to cross, not mine.

HIRSCHFELD: You mean, it is to be just us?

QURIE: With no moderator?

LARSEN: Out here, I will do all you ask. But in there, I cannot help you. Only you, together, can do this.

(The four men look at each other. They walk to the door. A moment, then Pundak steps forward and opens it. The others file in. As Pundak starts to close it behind him, he hesitates, eyes on Larsen, who shoos him in. The door closes.
Mona appears, speaking to Larsen as if on the phone.)

MONA: So, what do you think?

LARSEN: If Hassan Asfour does not kill us all in our sleep it will be a miracle.

And, Mona, this Ron Pundak! I mean, Hirschfeld is bad
enough—

MONA: I know, but Yossi personally selected these men.

LARSEN: Because the rest of his entire country was busy?
The Israelis should worry less about the PLO and more about
the judgment of their Deputy Foreign Minister.

*(Toril Grandal, the housekeeper, and her husband, Finn, the
groundsman, both fifties, enter carrying a heavy armchair and
a large rug.)*

MONA: Don't underestimate him. Yossi Beilin does everything for
a precise reason.

*(Larsen stops as he sees Toril and Finn begin to arrange the
furniture in the room.*
He moves toward the couple.)

LARSEN: No, no, no!
(Gesturing to move the couch)
They must be facing each other.

FINN *(In Norwegian)*: [Do you want me to bring in any / more
furniture?]

LARSEN: English only. We don't want our guests to think we are
keeping secrets.

TORIL *(Rough accent)*: Some English my husband understands, Mr.
Larsen, / but he speaks little.

LARSEN: Please: Terje. We are all friends here.
Now, did you get what I asked for?

TORIL: The Johnny Walker Black, yah.

LARSEN: Excellent. How many bottles?

FINN *(Holding up fingers)*: Four.

LARSEN: Get four *cases*.

*(He gestures to Finn. The two of them pick up the new armchair
and start to move it.)*

TORIL: I will serve herring to start.

LARSEN: Good.

TORIL: A small pasta course.

LARSEN: Excellent.

TORIL: And roasted pork stuffed with sage.

LARSEN *(Dropping the chair)*: No! For God's sake! Out of the question.

TORIL: But I have already / prepared the dish.

LARSEN: You will serve some fish? Yes? Salmon? Good.

TORIL: Mr. / Larsen—

LARSEN *(Cutting her off, snapping)*: JUST DO IT!

(He starts to exit, then stops. He turns around; all his charm again.)

My friends, you are a vital part of a grand undertaking. I will lean on you. I will rely on you. And I know you will rise to the occasion.

MONA *(To us)*: An hour passed as Terje waited. Then another hour. Then another, as the door stayed closed.

(The door to the room opens. Qurie strides out followed by Hirschfeld.)

QURIE: I must speak with Tunis. I require a phone.

TORIL: Follow me, sir, if you would.

(She leads Qurie off. Finn follows. Hirschfeld watches them go, then pulls Larsen close.)

HIRSCHFELD: They say they will take Gaza.
(Off Larsen's confusion) They propose Israel withdraw all forces from Gaza. That the territory be turned over to the Palestinians, who will govern it themselves. This is what Peres has been offering for years—*years*—but the Palestinians have always rebuffed. My God, to be able to pull out of Gaza—that would end the Intifada!

LARSEN: What did you offer in return?

HIRSCHFELD: Nothing! I can offer nothing. We are only / here to listen.

LARSEN: Of course. I understand.

HIRSCHFELD *(Pulling closer)*: They want to go even further. They have brought a draft of a Declaration of Principles.

(Off Larsen's look) A document that would spell out—precisely—the issues between us that both sides agree to address. They have come with a list of their issues, and they want to hear ours—now. What should I do?

LARSEN: That is not for me to say.

(Cutting him off before he can speak) Yair. Trust that you need no road map. The way will show itself.

HIRSCHFELD *(Stares, then)*: That is completely fucking stupid.

(He goes back into the room.
Mona appears, again on the phone.)

MONA: Terje.

LARSEN *(Out to her)*: I'm not coming back tonight. I have to stay.

MONA: You have a board meeting at Fafo tomorrow.

LARSEN: I don't have time for trivialities at a moment like this.

MONA: We can't have Marianne asking questions.

LARSEN: Tell her whatever, darling. You'll think of something. You always do.

The drawing room after dinner. The men sit by the fire, whiskey tumblers in hand as Larsen refills them. Qurie, tie loosened, sits near Hirschfeld and Pundak.
Asfour sits off to the side, watching, his tie still cinched.

QURIE: Dinner was excellent.

PUNDAK: Fantastic!

HIRSCHFELD: Our compliments to the chef!

LARSEN: But, Hassan, you barely touched your food.

QURIE: Hassan is from Gaza, where they are all fishermen but hate the sight of fish.

(As he shakes his tumbler at Larsen) No more, Larsen, no more.

(Hirschfeld and Pundak laugh—as they shake their tumblers at Larsen as well.)

PUNDAK: Yes, Terje, no more / for me too. Not even a drop.

HIRSCHFELD: I couldn't possibly have another sip.

(As Larsen elaborately refills their tumblers . . .)

LARSEN: And what about *your* father, Abu Ala?

PUNDAK: Yes, it's your turn. Tell us.

QURIE: Ah, now *there* is a man!

He was born in a village just outside Jerusalem. As a child he would take me to the Old City, where the very stones speak to you. Through the winding streets we would go, until we would emerge, stand before it, and he would say:

(As his father, pointing) "There—*there*—Ahmed, that is the Aqsa Mosque. The beating heart of Jerusalem. Wherever you go, boy, you must always hold it—and this city—here . . . *(Pointing to his heart)* . . . for it will always be your home."

He would sit me by his side and we would eat olives. He would tell stories. Politics. Food. Women.

I *hate* olives. Like stones in my mouth. But to keep him talking, I would eat and eat.

(They drink. Larsen turns to Asfour.)

LARSEN: And, finally, Hassan.

ASFOUR: The petty bourgeois construct of family does not interest me. The struggle against the Western capitalist behemoth: *that* is my father.

PUNDAK *(Jumping up)*: That's it! No more sourpuss from you!

(Slapping his hands together) Right. I have a joke.

HIRSCHFELD: Ron.

PUNDAK: No, listen! It's good, it's good. Here it is.

Interpol, the CIA, and Mossad are chasing a rabbit. They come to the edge of a forest. Interpol combs the forest; they cannot find the rabbit. The CIA burns *down* the forest, but still no rabbit. Then Mossad says, "Give us thirty minutes." They go off. Half hour later, they come back with a grizzly bear in a headlock, with a broken nose and black eye, and the bear is yelling: "Okay, I'm a rabbit! I'm a rabbit!"

(Wagging his finger at Asfour) Ah, Mr. Lenin likes the joke!

QURIE *(Rising to his feet)*: Ah, ah, ah! *I* will tell a joke!
A man is married forty years. Then, his wife, she dies. After the funeral, after all are gone, he sits alone in his house. The shadow of loneliness falls upon him. In his solitude, he cries out: "I am all alone! What will I do now?"
Again, he cries: "I am all alone! I have no wife! No one to tell me what to do! No one to tell me what to say!"
(Beat. A revelation. Eyes wide, hands in the air) "I am all alone!" *(Joyous, to the heavens)* "I am all alone!"

(Arms still raised, he bursts into a lumbering jig. All but Asfour clap in time as Qurie yells out in time to his dance:)

"I am all alone! I am all alone! I am all alone! Alone, alone, alone!"

(He ends with a flourish as Pundak thrusts his hands at him, fighting to get his words out as he laughs.)

PUNDAK: He . . . he . . . he looks like Arafat. When he . . . *(Mimicking Qurie's movements)* Those crazy Arafat gestures we see on TV.
QURIE: Do not insult the Chairman!
PUNDAK *(Shocked)*: I—I—I / am sorry.
QURIE: You insult the Chairman, you insult us!
PUNDAK: / Abu Ala, I did not mean to offend.
HIRSCHFELD: Ron gets excited. / He was just playing.
LARSEN: My friends, / let us all take a breath.
QURIE *(Roaring over them)*: You think we are just here as *us*? We are the head and arms of *him*!
ASFOUR *(In Arabic)*: [That is enough!]
QURIE *(Turning on him, in Arabic)*: [Do not interrupt! / I am your superior!]
LARSEN *(Over them all)*: Breathe! All of us!

(As Toril enters with plates of waffles, Qurie advances on Hirschfeld and Pundak.)

QURIE: We will bury you before you take our honor! We will break you!

TORIL: I have brought waffles.

QURIE *(To Toril; seamlessly switching gears)*: Ahhhh! There she is! The one I love is here! You spoil us. You are the hostess of all hostess.

LARSEN: Yes. Well. Let's all try them, shall we?

(He gestures to Toril: "Take the lead—now."
As Toril passes out plates of waffles to the men . . .)

TORIL: This is the waffle recipe of my mother. Passed on from her mother. It is simple but precise.

To make the batter, first you separate the eggs. Then the yolks must be beaten in a bowl, light and frothy. Then you add vanilla, then sugar, then butter, then buttermilk, then flour, and then the secret, which is the cardamom.

The egg whites are beaten separately and folded in. Then you cook the batter, hot and swift.

(Demonstrating) For the serving, you spread the whip cream . . . and the lingonberry . . . *Then . . .*

(Gesturing for them to do so) . . . you eat.

(As one, the men do. They chew. Then, as one, they loudly express their pleasure.)

(In Arabic): Shukran. [Thank you.]
(Then to the Israelis, in Hebrew) Toe dah. [Thank you.]

QURIE *(To Asfour, in Arabic)*: [Do you hear this one!]

PUNDAK *(To Toril, in Hebrew)*: [No, thank *you*!]

HIRSCHFELD *(To Toril, in Hebrew)*: [It is very nice of you.]

(She is gone, taking the merriment with her. Silence. Then . . .)

I propose that we agree that there are certain subjects— people—we do not discuss. Just as . . .

(Pointing to the door) when we are in there.

ASFOUR: Red lines. Which we do not cross.

HIRSCHFELD: Yes.

Here, let us be friends.

MONA *(To us)*: Two days and nights they worked, almost without stopping. Waffles, cigarettes, waffles, coffee, waffles. Behind closed doors without a road map. Hammering out a joint draft of a Declaration of Principles, known as a DOP—radical, without precedent—recognizing that each side had grievances. And both sides wished to find a way to find a way.

The entrance hall.
Larsen stands with the four guests, who wear winter coats and hold suitcases, mid-goodbyes to Toril and Finn.

LARSEN: Now for God's sake, make sure you leave nothing behind. No traces, yes?

TORIL: Mr. Hassan, was last night's venison to your liking?

ASFOUR: It was superb. Thank you, comrade.

You do not know it but, at heart, you are a communist.

QURIE *(To Toril)*: My sweet, return with me to Tunis. My wife will not mind.

TORIL *(Gesturing to Finn)*: But my husband might.

QURIE: He is a man of the West: they are flexible.

LARSEN: There is one last order of business: your code names. For the safety of *all* of you, from now on, when you are speaking on the phone . . .

(Gesturing to the professors) Israel will be referred to as "The Little Country." Prime Minister Rabin will be "The Grandfather," Shimon Peres "The Father," and Yossi Beilin "The Son."

(Gesturing to Qurie and Asfour) The PLO will be referred to as "Those Across the Sea." Chairman Arafat will *also* be a "Grandfather," and Abu Ala will be "Puntoffle."

QURIE: Wait.

I am to be called—*what*? "The Falafel"?

HIRSCHFELD: "Puntoffle," Abu Ala. It means "slipper," in Yiddish.

(Qurie stares at him.)

QURIE: You are an even stranger people than I imagined.
(Slapping his hands) Come. Let us all embark.

(With stiff formality, Asfour extends his hand to Hirschfeld.)

ASFOUR: May your travels be safe.
HIRSCHFELD *(Taking it)*: And yours.
ASFOUR *(As they shake . . .)*: You are my first Jew.
HIRSCHFELD: I hope I was not too stringy.
ASFOUR: A bit. But still better than fish.

(Qurie steps toward Pundak who steps back and points at the ground between them.)

PUNDAK: Ah! Red line!

(Laughter. Qurie claps Pundak's shoulder.)

QURIE *(To the group)*: This one! This one brings me joy!
(Calling after the Israelis as they leave) Be safe! Fly well!

A shift.
Larsen and Qurie alone.

QURIE: Larsen, look at them: they are the Laurel and the Hardy.
With them we can go no further.
LARSEN: Yair and Ron, they are not official but they are here *for*
the officials.
QURIE: We must deal directly with the Israeli Government. You
tell Yossi Beilin, I have put an offering on the table. I demand
a man of equal status be the one who responds.

Beilin appears.

MONA *(To us)*: Terje flew back immediately to Tel Aviv to meet
with Yossi Beilin. The same tandoori restaurant.
BEILIN *(As he eats)*: Yogurt?

LARSEN: No, thank you. Yossi, the progress that was made—in one two-day meeting—it is beyond imagination. And the Palestinians have told me they wish to return.

BEILIN: Excellent.

LARSEN: So then you must see that it is time to upgrade the Israeli delegation to official status.

BEILIN: Upgrade? Terje, Israel has no delegation *to* upgrade. That would be illegal.

LARSEN: Of course, but your professors—

BEILIN: *My* professors? I own them now.

LARSEN: Look, Yair and Ron are lovely and charming and semi-well-dressed, but they are not up to the task.

BEILIN: Their task is to listen and report back to me, which they have done very well.

LARSEN: Yossi, look at it from the other side. These are Ministers from the PLO who are risking their lives!

BEILIN: Which as Deputy Foreign Minister of the State of Israel is none of my concern.

(Cutting Larsen off before he can speak) If the Palestinians want to meet again in Oslo, then they will meet with Yair and Ron.

LARSEN: For God's sake, we have to give them *something!*

Let me *at least* tell them Peres is behind this.

(Beilin stares, saying nothing. Larsen stares back.)

He doesn't know?!

But . . .

Yossi.

You *told* me—

BEILIN: What? I told you what? Do you remember my precise words? Because I do.

When people talk to you, Terje, you should pay attention to what they actually say and not just listen for what you want to hear.

If and when something occurs in this Channel that I deem worthy enough to bring to the Foreign Minister's attention—then, he will know. For now I, and I alone, know. If the PLO want to continue, this is how it will go.

The Larsen flat. Egeland paces before Mona and Larsen.

EGELAND: My God! I mean, I mean—my God!

Here I am, worried the Palestinians are running a rogue operation; it turns out, it's the fucking Israelis.

LARSEN: Yes, well, things are a bit more complicated than we thought, but this is only a wrinkle.

EGELAND: A "wrinkle"?

(To Mona) Is he fucking serious?

(To Larsen) If Peres finds out what his so-called protégé is doing, he will tell *our* Foreign Minister.

LARSEN: It is not ideal, I agree, but Yossi *will* send Yair and Ron back here. Now I know what Abu Ala said, but *I* can get him to return as well. We must push on.

EGELAND *(To Mona)*: Really? *This* is who you ended up with?

(To Larsen) Do you even listen to what falls out of your mouth? Mona and I are government officials—who will be accused of conspiring with *another* government's official. We will be fired, jailed, worse!

(Cutting Larsen off before he can speak) We are done. We are pulling out—now.

MONA: Hold on.

(Both men turn and look at her.)

(Working it out) Beilin keeping Peres in the dark could be a very good sign.

The moment he upgrades the delegation, he will have to tell Peres. When Peres knows, *he* will have to tell Prime Minister Rabin. They hate each other. They have been rivals for thirty years. Anything Peres tells the Prime Minister, Rabin will be suspect of, in the extreme.

EGELAND: Ah.

I see.

(Unseen by Egeland, Larsen gestures to Mona: "I love you! I love you!")

(Working it out) Beilin protects Peres by not telling him till he has something concrete. Then, when he *has* to tell him, Peres will go to Rabin—

LARSEN: And Rabin will not cut down a tree that is bearing fruit.

MONA: *Might* not cut it down.

(To Egeland) I think we should push on.

(Silence. Egeland thinks. Mona and Larsen wait.)

EGELAND: One more meeting. Discreet. Under wraps.

LARSEN: Guaranteed.

Borregaard Estate. The negotiating room.
Cigarettes. Ashtrays. Coffee cups. Piles of paper.
Qurie and Asfour sit, each reading a copy of a document; a nervous Hirschfeld and Pundak stand, watching them. No one moves. Then, Qurie looks up.

QURIE: Where is your direct reply to our concrete offer to take control of Gaza?

HIRSCHFELD: We think, the draft of the DOP Ron and I have written—clearly—puts forward our *own* specific proposals.

QURIE: No, you put forward eloquent generalities.

My friends, this is our second round of meetings. Time is ticking.

Who will control security at border checkpoints?

What is to become of the illegal settlements you have built on our land?

(Hirschfeld and Pundak look at each other, then back to Qurie and Asfour.)

HIRSCHFELD: We . . . *can* acknowledge that . . . in unofficially speaking to . . . a person in a position to know . . . there is some interest in your Gaza offer.

QURIE: You are speaking of the man with whom you breakfast in Tel Aviv.

HIRSCHFELD: I did not say his name, Abu Ala.

QURIE: But you did not *not* say his name.

(They stare at each other.)

Good.

Now this is what we *further* propose for our joint document: that it officially, concretely addresses the status of the city of Jerusalem.

(Hirschfeld and Pundak look at him, stunned.)

HIRSCHFELD: Abu Ala.

Jerusalem?

QURIE: Of course. We cannot have a DOP that does not address our claim to our home. If we do not address *this* issue, what hope do we have for peace?

A crowd of Israeli Citizens fills one side of the stage, voices raised as one. Mona speaks to us.

ISRAELI CITIZENS *(In Hebrew)*: [Shut them out!]

MONA: March 1993. A Palestinian youth in Tel Aviv kills two Israelis.

ISRAELI CITIZENS *(In Hebrew)*: [Shut them out!]

MONA: In response, Prime Minister Rabin seals Gaza.

(A crowd of Palestinian Citizens fills the stage's other side.)

Forcing thirty thousand inhabitants out of work.

PALESTINIAN CITIZENS *(In Arabic)*: [Let us work!]

MONA: Two Palestinians are slaughtered.

PALESTINIAN CITIZENS *(In Arabic)*: [Let us work!]

MONA: An Israeli woman is hacked to death.

ISRAELI CITIZENS *(In Hebrew)*: [Shut them out!]

MONA: The calls to our flat were constant. They could not speak to each other so Terje became their intermediary.

The Larsen flat.

Larsen speaks on one phone as Mona listens to his conversation on another.

At the same time, Beilin is in his office in Jerusalem; Qurie is in his office in Tunis.

LARSEN: I understand—I more than understand, I empathize. But you must see that this action is counterproductive.

BEILIN: For God's sake! Our people are being murdered in the streets. If our Grandfather did not close the border he would have been hounded from office.

Tell Those Across the Sea that we are still willing to continue discussions. If Puntoffle will return for a third round, the Two Men from Haifa will return.

(Mona whispers in Larsen's ear. He repeats what Mona is telling him into the phone.)

LARSEN: . . . Let me speak frankly.

. . . Those Across the Sea are emphatic.

. . . They say the Little Country must upgrade its delegation.

BEILIN: You tell Puntoffle that *we* decide who we send. Tell him to tell *his* Grandfather that when he puts something on the table of substance, *then* we will consider his request.

QURIE *(To Larsen)*: We have put nothing *but* substance! We have offered to take Gaza off their hands! You tell the Son, we know that his Father Above Him has long pined for this.

We demand an upgrade as reciprocity!

BEILIN *(To Larsen)*: Those from Across the Sea are not in a position to make demands!

(Beilin is gone.)

QURIE: Fuck him! He is a fucking bastard! *We* are the ones risking without knowing whom we are risking to. *Our* lives hang in the balance! They will not upgrade, so I will not return!

LARSEN: They will!

MONA *(Hissing to him)*: Terje!

QURIE: They will?

LARSEN: Yes.

MONA: What are you doing?

QURIE: Who? Who are / they sending?

LARSEN: I don't know. Not the details. But an upgrade is coming.

QURIE: How do you know this?

LARSEN: Mona has told me.

She has met with the Son, from The Little Country. She has made him promise that if you return to Oslo and meet with the Men from Haifa one more time, then he will upgrade. Guaranteed.

QURIE *(Beat. Then . . .)*: Mona has done this?

LARSEN: Yes.

QURIE: Swear it to me, Larsen. On the soul of your wife.

LARSEN: I do.

(Qurie and Larsen stand, facing outward, phones gripped.)

Puntoffle, you must trust me.

QURIE: I trust Mona, Larsen. Without her, you are nothing. Book the flight.

(Qurie is gone.
Mona stands still. Staring at Larsen.)

LARSEN: Mona. He wants to come back. He *needed* me to tell him that. If there were another way / I would have chosen it.

MONA: What's the one thing, Terje. The one thing you said you / would not do.

LARSEN: Darling, for a negotiation to succeed, there must be constructive ambiguity, so / both sides may claim achievement.

MONA: I typed that lecture, Terje, don't read it back to me.

Do you understand what you've done? That you have made me culpable?

LARSEN: Darling, Yossi will upgrade.

MONA: How do you know that?

LARSEN: Because he will.

MONA: That is not an answer!

LARSEN: Mona, look at what is happening! All we've accomplished. / A hundred years of hate and bloodshed—teetering on the cusp of change!

We must do whatever it takes!

MONA: That you have now jeopardized by your recklessness. Your total disregard of everything we agreed to.

(In response to Larsen's last line above) Except lying to them, Terje! Only a bungling amateur lies!

LARSEN: God, you are so fucking Norwegian! Everything is an objection! Everything is a problem! I am on the phone with them, day and night, fighting to stay on my feet, and all you want is for me to sink to my fucking knees!

(Silence. Neither moves.)

Darling. I apologize.
Forgive me.

(Mona doesn't move.)

Mona. You know how I . . .
I meant none of it.
You—*you* are everything / to me.

MONA: Terje.
This all ends. Tomorrow.
Unless you do one thing.

LARSEN: Of course.
What?

MONA: Tell Holst what we are doing.

LARSEN: But but but but he's *Holst*.

MONA: And about to be Foreign Minister.

LARSEN: But he's a megalomaniac. The very fact he did not initiate—this alone will doom us.

MONA: Terje, you have compromised me. We must get Holst's support *before* he is responsible for the Ministry—for any mistakes *by* the Ministry—or my career is over.

And *if* we can get him on our side, that megalomania is exactly what we need.

(Larsen stares at her, trying to keep up.)

Holst does nothing in half measures. If we can convince him to keep the Channel open, when he takes office he will put the full weight of the Ministry behind it. I will be *officially* involved, and we *will* make this happen.

(They look at each other.)

LARSEN: You are the most extraordinary woman who has ever lived. / There are no *words* to describe how much I love you.
MONA: Terje. Terje. No. Not here. Not now.
I'll invite them to dinner this Sunday.
LARSEN: But Yossi and Abu Ala will both call.
MONA: Good. Then Holst will know we're not making this up. We'll pretend we got the time zones crossed. Better to throw him into it than try to explain.

Holst and Marianne appear in the positions they held at the end of the first scene.

MONA: You'll tell a story, then a toast, all to flatter Holst.

(They toast.)

LARSEN: What do you think he'll say?
MONA: He'll be a little upset.
HOLST: Fuck fuck fuck fuck fuck fuck fuck FUCK!
MONA: But he'll listen to reason.
HOLST: I forbid this! Do you understand me?
    (To Larsen) You are a fucking dilettante!
    (To Mona) You work for me!
    (To them both) And this is over!

ACT TWO

The stage is filled with bodies moving to and fro.
Qurie approaches Holst as Mona speaks to us.

MONA: Two days later. The bar of the Hotel Bristol in Oslo. I pressed
and Holst agreed to a meeting. Abu Ala came from Tunis. *He*
would convince Holst to back us, or we were done.

HOLST: What Terje has told me, this is all true? That Arafat is willing to risk dialogue with the Israeli Government?

QURIE: The Chairman is one thousand percent behind this back
channel. You have my word, upon the heads of my daughters.

HOLST: Who knows about this? *Exactly* who?

QURIE: Arafat, myself, and Hassan Asfour.

HOLST: Good.

QURIE: And the Jordanians.

HOLST: What?!?

(Larsen gestures to Qurie: "What are you doing?")

QURIE: The Chairman had no choice but to speak of this to King
Hussein.

HOLST *(To Larsen)*: Did you know this?! / Did you keep this from me as well?!

LARSEN: Johan Jorgen, I had no idea!

(To Qurie) Why would Arafat do such a thing?!

QURIE: The Jordanians are our patrons. To them, we can afford no secrets. For without their support, the PLO would cease to exist. But rest assured: when the Chairman is forced to speak of things he does not wish to . . .

(Leaning in) Believe me, he ensures that his words make no sense whatsoever.

HOLST: Look, what has happened so far—the violation of protocol has been totally inappropriate.

QURIE: I agree.

HOLST: My God, the risks. Not even a security detail.

QURIE: That was Larsen's idea.

HOLST: Driving alone, middle of the night—rental cars!

QURIE: Again, Larsen.

Minister Holst, in but two meetings, the Israelis and ourselves have made progress beyond all hopes. With your support, our secret tributary will continue to feed fresh water to the official Washington-sponsored talks, moving two peoples towards peace, and enshrining your name forever.

(Holst stares at him. Qurie stares back. Holst decides.)

HOLST: At all future meetings there will be an elite two-man security detail, chosen by me.

QURIE: Agreed.

HOLST: My Deputy, Jan Egeland, will run all further liaisons between you and your Israeli—

QURIE: No. It must be Larsen.

His ways are strange, but through his methods we have begun a *true* dialogue between our peoples.

If we are to succeed, it must be he. For this one speaks truth to both sides. He does not lie.

Do you, Larsen?

Thank you, Minister Holst. We *will* meet again.

Frogner Park, near the Hotel Bristol.
Larsen and Holst walk alone.

HOLST: He's holding something back.

LARSEN: Johan Jorgen, everything he said is true.

HOLST: But what did he *not* say? That's what concerns me.

LARSEN: I know this man. He can be trusted.

HOLST: Terje, he is the Finance Minister of the PLO. If you trust him, or the Israelis, you are an even bigger fool than I thought.

(They walk on.)

LARSEN: So, what do you think of all this?

HOLST: What do I *think*, Terje?

I think for months, you have looked Marianne in the face, you have looked *me* in the face, and you have lied.

LARSEN: Johan Jorgen, Mona told you why we / could not tell you.

HOLST: And you convinced a colleague—a trusted colleague—to keep me in the dark.

I underestimated you, Terje. I won't make that mistake again.

(And he's gone.)

MONA *(To Larsen)*: What did Holst say?

LARSEN Totally enthusiastic. Couldn't be happier.

Borregaard Estate. Drawing room.
Larsen seeks to calm a seething, pacing Qurie.

MONA *(To us)*: Two weeks later. Borregaard Castle.

QURIE: They have proposed *nothing*, Larsen.

In there, for two days and nights, those monkeys have weaved and bobbed and stalled—because they have no authority *to* propose.

This entire round, we have moved our document forward not one inch!

LARSEN: Abu Ala, please. You must go back in. Whatever Yair and Ron have proposed, it cannot be that bad. Trust the process. Move forward.

QURIE: I have upheld my end of the bargain. I have done as Yossi Beilin asked.

Now. He. Upgrades.

(Silence. The two men stare at each other.)

Upon her soul, you swore, Larsen.

To break an oath is a sin. For which men are punished.

Yossi Beilin appears.

LARSEN: Yossi. I beg you. You must listen to me. *Now* is the moment for bold and forthright—

BEILIN: Yeah, fine, I'll upgrade.

(Larsen stares at him, stunned.)

LARSEN: You . . . but . . . you—

BEILIN: Yair and Ron have taken things as far as they can; now it's time to make things official.

LARSEN: This this this is fantastic! Incredible!

How soon can you come to Oslo?

BEILIN: It won't be me. I'm identified too closely with Shimon. If we were ever to get to the point where we had enough to tell Rabin—the fact that it came from Shimon *and* me? He'll shut it down, two seconds flat.

LARSEN: Then who?

BEILIN: Just get them to agree to another round and we'll send a senior representative of the Israeli Government.

But if the Palestinians breathe a *word* about this—

LARSEN: Yossi, they will not do such a thing. They are committed to keeping the Channel secret. Arafat told me this, to my face.

BEILIN: With respect, Terje, put the word of Yasser Arafat in one hand and take a shit in the other, and I think you know which will have more weight.

Tell them, one word and we are done.

A cocktail reception.
Waiters pass champagne to the delegates, diplomats, and journalists.
Larsen and Mona are on one side of the room, drinks in hand.

LARSEN: Mona! The upgrade is happening!

MONA: I know. I can't believe it. It's fantastic.

(An American Diplomat on the other side of the room spies Larsen and yells across.)

AMERICAN DIPLOMAT: Terje! *(Mispronounces it "TUR-juh")*

LARSEN *(To Mona)*: So who do you think the Israelis are going to send?

AMERICAN DIPLOMAT: Hey, Terje! *(Mispronounces it again)*

MONA *(Realizing; sotto)*: Terje, I think that's you.

LARSEN *(Sotto, in turn)*: Seriously?

AMERICAN DIPLOMAT: Good to see you here!

LARSEN *(Loudly, waving)*: And you!

(To Mona) Who is he?

AMERICAN DIPLOMAT: How are the secret negotiations going?

(Silence—a switch flicked—Larsen and Mona are deer in head-lights, all eyes on them.)

LARSEN: Sorry?

AMERICAN DIPLOMAT: The back channel negotiations. How'er they going? Give me the play-by-play.

LARSEN: I'm not quite sure what you're referring to.
Negotiations? No, I don't—news to me.

AMERICAN DIPLOMAT: Ah, come on.

LARSEN: No, really, it's just a complete mystery, what you are saying, and I think—ah, yes! There's my friend. So good to chat. Be well.

(As Larsen starts to go . . .)

AMERICAN DIPLOMAT: Larsen.
I asked you a question.
Tell me what's going on.

Oslo. The Foreign Ministry.
Holst paces before Egeland, Mona, and Larsen.

HOLST: How the hell did the Americans find out?!

MONA: We don't know. But, clearly, one of the parties involved leaked it. The question is who?

EGELAND: What if . . .
What if *we* leaked it?

(Holst stops. He turns and looks at Egeland.
Mona and Terje stare at him as well.)

I was in Washington, two months ago, at the State Department. I made a casual mention of what we were doing. Slipped it in. Among other remarks. I thought they weren't paying attention.

HOLST: You just "slipped it in"?!

EGELAND: Johan Jorgen, this was what we had decided to do, *before* you were appointed.

MONA: What's important, is that no one higher up on the American side knows. I've checked, Johan Jorgen: the information has not been passed up the chain. For now, the leak is contained.

HOLST: I see. So. Someone in Washington just wants us to know they know. A shot across our bow.
Put us in our place. Let us know—once again—that they are bigger and better than us.
Well *fuck them*. Fuck the State Department, fuck Warren Christopher—*I* run the foreign policy of this country.
(Beat. Then) We stay the course. For now.
But if one more leak is sprung—*just one*—I will shut this Channel down.

Larsen and Yossi Beilin face outward.

BEILIN: Terje, I've selected who's coming.

LARSEN: Fantastic! Who is it, Yossi?

(Uri Savir, thirties, appears in a tailored black suit, black shirt, and black sunglasses.)

BEILIN: Uri Savir.

Director-General of our Foreign Ministry.

LARSEN: What kind of man is he?

BEILIN: He's the man for the job.

LARSEN: But is he committed to the Oslo process? Does he understand the *delicacy* of—

BEILIN: Terje.

That's not your concern.

(Savir stands still, staring outward, face like stone.)

Fornebu Airport. The waiting area for international arrivals. Night.
The lounge teems with passengers traveling to and fro.
Larsen, Hirschfeld, and Pundak scan the faces of the passengers disembarking.
Off to the side stand two Norwegian men in dark suits.
Savir enters.

PUNDAK: There he is!

(Pundak waves. Savir stops walking and "inspects" his watch.
Larsen, Hirschfeld, and Pundak cross to Savir, who does not look up.)

LARSEN: Welcome, / welcome!

HIRSCHFELD: Such a pleasure to meet you. / An honor. Truly.

PUNDAK: Nice to have another "professor" with us, anh?

(All three men extend their hands. Savir doesn't extend his.)

SAVIR *(To Larsen)*: Your security detail is calling attention. Send them on ahead.

(Larsen and the professors look at each other. They withdraw their hands.)

LARSEN: Of course. As you wish.

(He nods to the two men in dark suits. They turn and exit. He turns back to Savir.)

Shall we get your bags?

SAVIR: I don't have any bags. I have thirty-six hours.

HIRSCHFELD: Are there any details you'd like us to brief you on? Obviously, a great distance still to go but as you know from Yossi, the progress, it's been dizzying.

PUNDAK: We should be sitting down. Ha!

(Savir stands still, staring at them. Then:)

SAVIR: I have to take a piss.

(And Savir is gone.)

PUNDAK: Terje, what is his problem?

HIRSCHFELD: Why is he acting / like this?

LARSEN: My friend. My friends.
He is nervous, we are nervous; it will all work out.

Borregaard Estate. Reception area. That night.
Mona, Hirschfeld, Pundak, Qurie, and Asfour.
Savir enters with Larsen.
Silence.
Qurie and Asfour stare at Savir.

LARSEN: Well, here we all are, safe and sound.
(Gesturing to Qurie and Asfour) Uri Savir, meet Abu Ala, terrorist number one, and Hassan Asfour, terrorist number two.
(To them, gesturing to Savir) And here is the man who wants to kill you.

(No one laughs. No one moves.)

MONA: Mr. Savir, it's a pleasure to meet you, and to have you as our guest. I hope you, like these four gentlemen, will not hesitate to ask for our assistance in any matter, no matter how small.

(Savir looks at Mona. He takes off his sunglasses.)

SAVIR: Thank you.

(Savir turns his head and stares at Qurie and Asfour.)

I am here at the personal request and as the voice of Shimon Peres.

(The room absorbs this. Qurie's gaze stays locked on Savir.)

QURIE: And I am here at the personal request and as the voice of Yasser Arafat.

*(They stare at each other. No one moves.
Qurie extends his hand.)*

Welcome to Oslo.

(Beat. Eyes locked. Savir extends his hand. They shake.)

MONA *(To us)*: Two men, in a room, extend their hands and history begins to change.

SAVIR: I have things to say.

QURIE: As do we.

SAVIR *(Pointing to the door)*: Let us begin.

*(Savir gestures: "After you."
Asfour crosses to the door and opens it. Qurie enters the room; Asfour follows suit.
Hirschfeld and Pundak enter the room as well.
Savir crosses to the door, nods at Mona, stares at Larsen . . . then closes it behind him.
The two dark-suited Norwegian Secret Service Agents from the airport enter.)*

LARSEN: Ah, gentlemen!

So sorry. If you could, once again, your names?

TROND: I am Trond.

THOR: And I am Thor.

MONA *(To us)*: You cannot make these things up.

LARSEN: My friends, I wanted to have a moment alone with you, for you are now a vital part of a grand undertaking.

(The two men stare at Larsen. They say nothing; they don't move.)

For you to contribute fully, you must socialize with us.

You must eat with us. You must drink with us.

THOR: Yah, / we can do that.

TROND: That will be fine.

THOR: One of us on duty, one of us off, at all times.

LARSEN: Wonderful. Now as you have—undoubtedly—never personally been assigned a mission of this gravity and complexity, allow me to educate you as to who these men are.

THOR: Ahmed Qurie, born March 26, 1937, near Jerusalem. Reports to Chairman Yasser Arafat, who has ordered multiple assassinations on Norwegian soil, all of which I have *personally* stopped.

TROND: Hassan Asfour, studied in Moscow at Patrice Lumumba University, where, according to my *personal* investigation, he was recruited to spy for the Soviets.

(Beat. Larsen blinks.)

THOR: Now, if you will excuse us, we need to reinspect the premises.

(Thor and Trond are gone.
Larsen and Mona are alone. As one, they turn and stare at the closed door.)

MONA *(To us)*: And then we waited.

(Beat. Again, as one, they look at the door.)

(To us) And waited.

LARSEN: Oh, for God's sake! Are they peeing in their coffee cups? When are they going to—

(The door opens. Larsen and Mona freeze.
Qurie, Asfour, and Savir exit the room, followed by the professors.
The men all stand still, staring at Larsen.)

QURIE: It is over. We return to Tunis.
These meetings, our work, it is erased.
(Beat. Then, whirling on Larsen) Aaaaah! Got you!

(All five men who were in the room burst into laughter.)

(Pointing at Larsen) Look at him! Look at him!
(To Savir) You were right.
PUNDAK: Terje! Your face, it was like: "Waaaaah!"

(Larsen and Mona stare, still digesting.
Savir turns to Qurie; formal now, with respect.)

SAVIR: Until tomorrow.
QURIE: Indeed.

(Savir walks toward the door. He stops. He turns back.)

SAVIR *(To Larsen and Mona)*: Are you two coming or not?
MONA *(To us)*: Terje and I drove him back to Oslo. He was ada-
mant he stay the night at our flat. Convinced he would be
recognized at *any* hotel. Because, as you know, every mid-
level Israeli diplomat is a rock star in Norway.

The Larsen flat. Late that night.
Savir and Mona and Larsen, half-empty champagne flutes in hand.
Savir regales them like a man unchained: light on his feet, ebullient,
bursting with energy.

SAVIR: I told everyone in my office, I'm off to Paris for the week-
end. I land at de Gaulle, take the car to the hotel, put the

do-not-disturb sign on the door, climb out the window, and head back to the airport, incognito.

And this is the best part: the flight from Paris here to Oslo? Completely packed. With Iranians. Me, the Director-General of the *Israeli* Foreign Ministry, trapped for two hours with two hundred sons of Persia.

LARSEN: What did you do?

SAVIR: What do you think I did? I shit my pants.

(Raising his glass) This is fantastic, by the way.

(To Mona) If your husband's diplomatic skills are half as good as his cellar, you should make *him* your Foreign Minister.

MONA: Oh, no, not Terje. He abhors the limelight.

LARSEN: Well, after all, what is a throne but a stool covered in velvet?

SAVIR *(To him, in French)*: [Aaaaah. A fellow admirer of Napoleon. Have you read his maxims in the original French?]

LARSEN *(In French, halting)*: [Yes. But. Many. Years ago.]

MONA: Napoleon.

SAVIR: Yes, that's one of his most famous maxims.

MONA: Terje has always told me it was his.

SAVIR: Well, you know how men are.

MONA: Yes, I do.

SAVIR: My God, this day! Life is nothing if not surprising, eh?

I mean, here I am with you, and two days ago I knew nothing about any of this, and two *weeks* ago I was running our consulate in New York.

(To Mona) Have you been?

MONA: New York? No, / I've not had a chance to go.

SAVIR: Oh, you must! My God, what a city. I mean, the jazz! The best places to hear it—in the world. Every night, I would go out: jazz, films, dancing—

(To Mona) Do you dance?

LARSEN: We both do.

MONA: Terje taught me.

SAVIR: Let me guess. The tango.

LARSEN: Yes, / that's right.

MONA: How did you know?

SAVIR: The hips. They never lie.

LARSEN: It's so interesting because, as a young man, I was a competitive / ballroom dancer.

SAVIR: You and I, Mona, we will have to dance.

MONA: You tango as well?

SAVIR: Promise me a dance, and you'll see.

Do you promise?

MONA: Do you ever take no for an answer?

SAVIR: Well, as they say, "Fortune is like a woman: only the audacious win her love."

LARSEN: Ah, Machiavelli. With my wife. How nice.

So, Uri, tell us: why *did* you leave New York?

SAVIR: Shimon asked me to return to Israel and serve by his side.

He called and said—

(As Peres) "This reminds me of a story. You'll find it very interesting."

That's how he starts *every* conversation.

Shimon Peres is a giant among men. Like a father to me. But, my God, the man takes *forever* to get to his point!

Finally he says—

(As Peres) "Come home, Uri. Your country needs you. *I* need you."

How could I say no?

And *now* he has selected me to do this.

(Slapping his hands together) God, I'm starving!

No, no, stay. Sit. I'll rummage. Pour some champagne.

(As Savir exits, Larsen calls after him:)

LARSEN: Of course. As you wish!

(Then, to Mona) I liked him so much better when he wasn't talking.

SAVIR *(Yelling, from offstage)*: I'll tell you a secret. I was nervous as hell to meet those two. The first members of the PLO I've ever been face-to-face with.

LARSEN *(Calling off)*: So what do you think of them?

SAVIR: Not the demons I was expecting.

This Ahmed— What do you call him?

MONA: Abu Ala.

(Savir enters, eating, more food in hand.)

SAVIR: I can do business with this man.
(He stops, shaking his head) My God. You can't imagine.
To have someone—*finally*—we can deal with.
I have thought of this day for . . . years.

LARSEN *(Raising his glass)*: A toast then.

MONA *(Raising hers)*: Yes.

SAVIR *(And he his)*: Absolutely.

LARSEN: To the—

SAVIR: I'm sorry, did you not ask for a toast?

LARSEN: . . . Pardon?

SAVIR: You asked for a toast.
(To Mona) He did, yes?
(To Larsen) So let me toast.

LARSEN: Ah. Yes. What I meant was—

SAVIR: You asked for a toast. So I am going to toast. What is the problem?

(No one moves. Larsen smiles.)

LARSEN: None at all.

(He gestures to Savir: "Be my guest.")

SAVIR *(Glass raised high)*: To new friends. And to the future.
May it be different. And may it come soon.

A phone rings.
Mona, alone, speaks out to us.

MONA: Al-lo?

(Egeland appears, speaking out to us as well.)

EGELAND: It's me. I need you here at the Ministry now.

MONA: Jan—

EGELAND: There's been another leak. My press secretary just called, in a panic. Agence France-Presse is reporting a secret Norwegian channel between Israel and the PLO. A small piece, buried, but *our* press have read it and they want to know what the fuck is going on.

You and I have to figure out how we're going to break this to Holst.

MONA: You haven't told him yet?

EGELAND: No, I called you first.

MONA: Good. We're not going to tell him.

(Silence. They stare outward.)

EGELAND: . . . Mona.

MONA: Because this isn't a problem. If it were, it would be our *duty* to tell him. But this is not.

Have your press secretary release a statement: this is all a misunderstanding. Agence France-Presse is *clearly* referring to the meeting on the Palestinian refugee situation that we— officially and openly—are about to host.

EGELAND: And the next leak? Because you know there will be one.

MONA: And we will deal with it then.

(Silence.)

We are not lying, Jan. We are choosing our words carefully.

(Neither moves.)

Please. Do this for me.

Borregaard Estate. Reception room. The next morning.
Savir stands with Hirschfeld and Pundak. Qurie and Asfour are across from them, as Qurie gestures to Toril and Finn who stand in the entranceway.

QURIE: Come, come!

(To Savir) You must meet our precious host and hostess. This is—

SAVIR: Toril, of course. And Finn.

(To them, in Norwegian) [Good morning. It is nice to meet you.]

TORIL *(To Finn, in Norwegian)*: [Did you hear that?]

FINN *(To Savir, in Norwegian)*: [The pleasure is ours.]

HIRSCHFELD: You speak Norwegian?

SAVIR: A few sentences. Picked them up on the plane.

(To Qurie) In our business, one must always be prepared.

QURIE: You do not know things, because you are new here, but *this* one, you will discover, cooks like those from above. Do I lie, Hassan?

ASFOUR: Comrade Toril is to food as Vladimir Lenin is to land reform.

SAVIR *(To Toril)*: Then I await tonight's meal with feverish anticipation.

(He bows to her, takes her hand, and kisses it. She beams. Qurie does not.

The door to the room opens and Larsen strides out.)

LARSEN: Ah, good. You're all here.

Mona sends her regards. She will join us for dinner.

The room is prepared for today's session.

(To Asfour) Dunhill cigarettes . . .

(To Qurie) Turkish coffee . . .

(To them all) . . . and copies of the current draft of the DOP.

QURIE: Is my coffee sweetened, Larsen?

LARSEN: Of course.

SAVIR: Pens and pads of paper?

LARSEN: As requested.

SAVIR: Good.

(To Hirschfeld and Pundak) You two are taking notes from now on.

(Silence. Everyone stares at Savir.)

HIRSCHFELD: But . . . Ron and I . . . we are the ones, with Abu Ala and Hassan, who created this draft document.

SAVIR: And I've read it and I'm up to speed.

HIRSCHFELD: Yossi has *explicitly* instructed us about our duties. I, I must insist that we be allowed / to participate.

(Savir points behind Hirschfeld.)

SAVIR: Oh! Look! Look over there! It's Yossi Beilin!
Oh, no. I was wrong. He's not here.
I am here. And I am in charge.

(No one moves.
Savir turns to Qurie. He gestures toward the door to the negotiating room.)

After you.

(Qurie and Hassan look at Savir. Then they look at Hirschfeld and Pundak . . .
Then they turn and walk into the room.
A moment. Then Hirschfeld walks into the room, followed by Pundak.
Savir follows them. He looks at Larsen. He winks. He closes the door.)

In the negotiating room.
Savir stands on one side of the room, Hirschfeld and Pundak seated behind him, pens and paper in hand. Facing them, on the other side of the room, are Qurie and Asfour.
Savir picks up a copy of the DOP.

SAVIR *(To Qurie)*: This DOP, the idea of it was yours, yes?
QURIE: Yes, it was.
SAVIR: It is nonbinding, of course, but we are willing to reference it as we go forward.
QURIE: This Declaration of Principles is not a reference. It is a road map, forged by both sides.
(Pointing to it) What is your official response to our concrete proposals therein?

SAVIR: I have no response to an unofficial document. What I have is a mandate to negotiate—in full—with you.

What you have all done in this room so far is discuss the *idea* of peace. I have been sent here to try and negotiate an *actual* peace.

So, let us put our cards on the table.

In my country, we see you as terrorists and murderers who wish to drive us into the sea.

You have killed our athletes in Munich, murdered our schoolchildren in Ma'alot, invaded us and spilled our blood on Yom Kippur, the highest holy day we have, and you call—daily—for our extermination. So you will understand when I say that we do not view you as ideal partners for peace.

QURIE: Mr. Savir, in my country, we see you as a savage nation whose army shoots our children for sport. *Your* people—persecuted for your faith, murdered in pogroms—fled to Palestine, where you were met with open arms, and left alone to pray and strive and grow strong. And when you *became* strong, you burned our homes, drove a million peoples *from* Palestine, and claimed—to this day—that there was never such a thing *as* Palestine.

So you will understand our mistrust of *you* as "ideal partners for peace."

(No one moves. Then:)

SAVIR: Well, now that we've both swung our dicks, let me say this: we are tired of being at war with you. We are committed to ending this cycle of violence and enmity. But I want to be clear. Israel will not sacrifice its security.

QURIE: And you will never have that security, Mr. Savir, until you make peace with us. For our region of the world will never accept you until *we* accept you.

(Savir picks up a copy of the DOP.)

SAVIR: Much of this we are willing to discuss. But first you must remove your demands in here that you know are impossible.

QURIE: I can think of no demands we have made that are not eminently possible.

SAVIR: Israel will not negotiate—in this room, or in any document—over the sovereignty of the city of Jerusalem.

QURIE: We will never relinquish our right to Jerusalem, just as we will never relinquish our right to a Palestinian State.

SAVIR: The possibility of a Palestinian State—without Jerusalem as its capital—is a viable topic, *if* you are willing to drop your further impossible demand that all issues not resolved in this DOP be referred to third-party international arbitration.

QURIE: You are Goliath to our David; the disparity of power between us is beyond measure. / A neutral arbitrator *is* essential.

SAVIR: All right. Okay. Listen. Give me *one* country that voluntarily cedes national sovereignty like you are proposing we do.

QURIE: The newly formed European Union comes to mind.

SAVIR: Not those fucking pansies, I mean a *real* country.

You see my point?

We've both got to be flexible here. Otherwise we are just pissing on each other's shoes, and I only brought one pair, anh?

ASFOUR: When one travels, comrade, packing too lightly can be dangerous.

SAVIR *(To Asfour)*: Is that like—what?—one of those pointless Arab sayings? Because I have no fucking idea what that means.

(To Qurie) We can talk in circles, or we can start to get something done.

Now, we are willing to relinquish control of Gaza—

QURIE: Which we will accept, on condition that you relinquish control of Jericho to us at the same time.

(Savir stares at him.)

SAVIR: Are you fucking serious?

QURIE: Gaza alone would make us an island surrounded by a sea of Israeli forces. We must have Jericho as well, for our protection.

SAVIR: I have been talking of nothing but Israel's concern for our security, and now you are asking us to give you control of a city twenty kilometers / from Jerusalem?

QURIE: I am talking about *our* city in *our* West Bank. *Your* country divides my people in two. So we must have a foothold in Gaza *and* the West Bank.

SAVIR: We'll give you Gaza, and when you show you can stop the killing of our soldiers *in* Gaza, then we will talk about Jericho. *(Cutting Qurie off before he can speak)* That is from Shimon Peres himself. Take it or leave it.

QURIE: I leave it. And when you and Peres come to your senses, it will be there for you to pick up, revise, and re-offer.

SAVIR: The offer is Gaza and Gaza only.

QURIE: Mr. Savir, perhaps in Tel Aviv, giving orders and negotiating are seen as one and the same. But in Tunis, we understand the difference.

(Savir and Qurie stare at each other.)

SAVIR: Abu Ala. We are going to have an interesting time together.

A shift. Later.
Larsen and Mona, alone. They face outward.

LARSEN: Mona! Where *are* you?

MONA: I'm on my way, I'll be there soon.

LARSEN: But you were to be here before dinner and it is almost midnight!

MONA: Terje, there are other crises in the world that / I have to deal with.

LARSEN: Darling, listen to me. Abu Ala and Uri—it is like dealing with two bulls in one china shop. They are knocking back whiskeys, they are pawing the earth, and things are getting a little— *(Fluttering his hand)* la la la.
I need you here. *Now.*

Borregaard Estate. Later that night. The drawing room.
Savir is mid-story, surrounded by Hirschfeld and Pundak, Qurie and Asfour, and Larsen and Thor—all with glasses of whiskey.

SAVIR: Kissinger is standing, right there—in the palace, in Beijing, this momentous summit—just he and Mao.

(To Qurie) This is the *other* Chairman, Abu Ala.

(Laughter as Qurie points his index finger to his eye and then at Savir.)

Everyone else is gone. They're the only ones left. And Mao, he is *staring* at him—eyes locked.

PUNDAK: My God, what did Kissinger do?

SAVIR: Exactly what *I* asked him. You know what he told me?

(As Kissinger) "Well, Uri, I met his gaze and I said, 'Mr. Chairman, as a fellow student of history, what do you think is the most important lesson of the French Revolution?'"

Mao stares back, and do you know what he said?

"Too soon to tell."

Anh? Anh? I mean, come on! For a communist, that is not fucking bad!

HIRSCHFELD: How do you know Kissinger, Uri?

SAVIR: Shimon introduced us. Now, Kissinger and I, we get together, we talk, we drink, we drink some more. It's a hard life, but someone has to do it.

THOR: I know Kissinger.

When he comes to Norway, I run his security detail.

PUNDAK: So? / And? Tell us.

HIRSCHFELD: What do you think of him, Thor?

(Thor looks at Larsen.)

LARSEN: Absolute discretion—guaranteed.

THOR *(To the room)*: What a fucking asshole.

(Laughter; whoops of delight.)

SAVIR: You say that, my friend, but there's not a man in this room who doesn't want an asshole as big as his.

(Raising his glass) To Kissinger's asshole: one day, may all of ours be so deep and wide!

ALL THE MEN (*Glasses raised*): Deep and wide!

(*As Mona bustles in . . .*)

Mona!

MONA (*To them all*): I'm so sorry. Work. Will you forgive me?

QURIE: It is already done!
(*To the men, pointing to Mona*) This one is like a daughter to
me; I hold her in my heart.

MONA (*To Savir*): How was dinner?

SAVIR: Abu Ala was right. That woman is a national treasure.

QURIE: Ah, just you wait. For now we are approaching the hour
of the waffles!
(*To the men*) Come! We must toast Mona!

(*The men rise to their feet with exuberance.*)

HIRSCHFELD: / Absolutely! We must!

PUNDAK: Yes, let's give her a cheer!

(*As Mona starts to protest—*)

SAVIR: No, no, no: we are going to praise you, you cannot stop us!

(*Qurie and the other men raise their glasses as one.*)

QURIE: To Mona. Without her, we are nothing.

ALL THE MEN: To Mona!

MONA (*To us*): The next morning. Only a few working hours
remained before Uri would have to rush back to Paris and
then to Jerusalem to keep his cover story intact.
The clock ticked. They pushed on.

The next morning. Borregaard Estate. The drawing room.
As Toril and Finn arrange the room—the door to the negotiating room
flies open and Qurie storms out.
Savir comes out, followed by Asfour and Hirschfeld and Pundak—
notepads in hand.

QURIE: I am packing my bags!

SAVIR: Abu Ala, we don't have time for this. My flight leaves in two hours.

QURIE: And by then we will be gone!

(Hirschfeld gestures to Toril: "Go get Terje now!"
As Finn and Toril leave . . .)

SAVIR: I have been blunt and honest, as a sign of my respect. And I give you my word that we will / consider this.

QURIE: Your word is written on ice, under the sun!
Yesterday, in there, you said, "The eventuality of a Palestinian State / is a viable topic for this discussion."

SAVIR: I did not . . . I did not!
"*Possibility* of a Palestinian State" is what I said.
(To Pundak) Why are you still writing?!

PUNDAK: But you said my job is now to / record minutes.

SAVIR: There, we are negotiating; here, we are off the record: learn the fucking difference!

(Larsen and Mona enter, followed by Toril and Finn.)

LARSEN: My friends, please! Lunch is about to be served. It is never good / to argue on an empty stomach.

SAVIR *(To Qurie)*: You want to discuss the *idea* of the eventuality of a Palestinian State? Then first you must address our security concerns.

QURIE: Your "concerns" are demands, and I will not / be demanded to.

SAVIR: We must have proof that the PLO will cease all terrorist / activities against all Israeli citizens.

ASFOUR *(To Qurie, in Arabic)*: [He is exactly as I told you he would be. / Give in on nothing else.]

SAVIR: Hassan, I'm right here! You want to say something about me, say it *to* me. We are here—finally—to speak to each other, yes? So be a man and do it!

ASFOUR: You stand there, comrade, with your colonial superiority, dictating what our future will or will not be. Yet somehow with your intelligence service, your army, your nuclear weapons—*you* are threatened by *us*.

So are you the master who must be obeyed or the victim who must be coddled? Because you cannot be both!

SAVIR: Tell me, Hassan, did you get those talking points mailed to you from Moscow or did you copy them down yourself?

ASFOUR: / *Your* future will be dictated by *us*! Your nation is surrounded by three-hundred-fifty million of *us*!

QURIE: Do not impugn this man's integrity!

SAVIR: If you think we are going to roll over on the issue of our security, you are sorely mistaken!

QURIE: You will have no security until we have our dignity!

SAVIR: Until we have security, you will have nothing!

(Simultaneously) You are wallowing in your grievances, just like always!

QURIE *(Simultaneously)*: Now you reveal your true face! Now we see the scoundrel you are!

(Larsen steps forward and puts his hand on Qurie's shoulder. Qurie whirls on Larsen with a roar, arm raised to hit him. He freezes, arm in mid-air. No one moves. Finally . . .)

(To Mona) Forgive my outburst. It was unworthy.

(She stares at him. Silence.)

Please allow me to make amends.

(Mona gestures with her head toward Savir. Realizing what she means, Qurie gestures back: "No, not that." She repeats the gesture more forcefully: "Yes, that!")

(Turning to Savir) Perhaps you and I . . .

(Mona gestures to Qurie with her fingers: "Take a walk.")

. . . could walk. Together.

If you wish.

The estate grounds, moments later.
As snow falls, Qurie and Savir walk together.
Behind them, at a discreet distance, Larsen and Mona follow.

QURIE *(Not looking back)*: Are they still following us?
SAVIR *(The same)*: Yes.
QURIE: They are like the KGB those two.
SAVIR: I was thinking Mossad.
QURIE: No, they are not *that* good.
SAVIR: I thought you were *really* going to hit him. That would have made my day.
QURIE: Believe me, whenever I am with Larsen, I wish to hit him.

(They walk on in silence. Then:)

SAVIR: I admire the way you fight.
QURIE: Thank you.
I admire . . . your passion.
SAVIR: My daughter says, with me, "passion" is another word for "pigheaded."
QURIE: Some men are like this. So I have heard.
SAVIR: She says, "Papa, all you care about is being right." I say, "Maya, if a man does not fight for what he believes, who is he?"

(Qurie stops. Savir follows suit.
Behind them, so do Larsen and Mona.)

QURIE: Maya.
SAVIR: Yes, my daughter.
QURIE: *My* daughter is named Maya. My youngest. She is the light of my life.

(They stare at each other.
They start walking again.
So do Larsen and Mona.)

SAVIR: I wish my father had lived to see this.

You and me, here.

Though he would not have been crazy about the weather.

QURIE: It is a true tragedy that we were approached by the Norwegians and not the Californians.

LARSEN: Mona, look at them. My God, they're smiling!

MONA: Hang back, Terje, let them be.

SAVIR: Is your father still with us?

QURIE: My father lives in Abu Dis, near Jerusalem.

SAVIR: Do you want me to take a letter to him? Give him a message from you?

QURIE: No. On the day I am able to leave Tunis and return home, *that* is the day he and I will speak.

But thank you.

(They stop walking.
So do Larsen and Mona.)

SAVIR: I want this to work. Shimon wants this to work. More than I can convey.

QURIE: As does the Chairman. And I.

MONA: Terje, if you take one step further, I *will* divorce you.

QURIE: We cannot escape each other, yours and mine. We are twined. This is our fate.

SAVIR: Abu Ala, our peoples live in the past—both obsessing over what we have lost.

Let us find a way to live in the present, together.

(They stare at each other.
Mona and Larsen stand frozen, watching.)

QURIE: We will agree to drop our demand that outstanding quarrels between us be referred to third-party international arbitration.

SAVIR: And we will agree to negotiate turning over Gaza *and* Jericho.

(Moving closer) Now, I will go home and tell Peres that you told me to go fuck myself. You go home and tell Arafat I said

the same. Then, in two days, I will have Terje call you and say we agree to your demands.

QURIE: And I will call him and do the same.

SAVIR: This way, both our bosses / get a victory.

QURIE: Yes, yes—we will go home and seduce them.
Perhaps that is not the correct use of this word.

SAVIR: My friend, that is exactly what we are going to do.
(Extending his hand) You and I, Abu Ala, we are going to change the world.

(Qurie takes Savir's hand and the two men stand there, eyes locked, hands gripped, as Larsen and Mona watch.)

ACT THREE

Joel Singer, forties, wearing a suit and tie, holds a copy of the draft of the DOP.

SINGER: What the fuck is this?!
MONA *(To us)*: Joel Singer, decorated veteran of the Israeli army.
SINGER: Who the fuck negotiated this?!
MONA *(To us)*: Now, senior law partner in a firm in Washington, DC.

In diplomacy, when the lawyers are called in, you know it's serious.

Jerusalem. Private conference room in the Foreign Ministry.
Singer, document in hand, stands before Savir and Beilin.

SAVIR: *You* try negotiating this.
SINGER: Negotiate? Uri, this is capitulate!
BEILIN: It's a working document.
SINGER: It's a fucking Hanukkah present to Yasser Arafat!

SAVIR *(To Beilin)*: Tell him! Tell him how much better this is, with *my* involvement.

(To Singer) Joel, this is after I walked it back. You don't want to know what we'd agreed to before I got involved.

SINGER: "Before you got involved"?

BEILIN: The first drafts were overseen by . . . nongovernmental agents.

SINGER: Who?

BEILIN: Two professors. Of economics.

From Haifa.

SINGER: Are you fucking serious?!

BEILIN: Joel, we had to start the process with no official contact. There *had* to be a firewall.

SINGER: So you picked men who were completely out of their league?

BEILIN: Joel, when we started this we didn't even know there *was* a league. We were fishing in the dark.

SINGER: I don't fish, Yossi, and neither should either of you—not with Israel's national security.

I mean, for God's sake—if you are even *entertaining* the idea of brain surgery, the one thing you do is make sure whoever picks up the knife is an actual fucking surgeon!

SAVIR: This is what Shimon wanted!

SINGER: Fuck Shimon! Shimon answers to Yitzhak—just like the rest of us.

(He holds up the DOP) This flies in the face of forty years of Israeli policy.

(Flicking through) We turn over control of Gaza *and* Jericho.

(Cutting them off before they can speak; reading) "The inclusion of Jerusalem in Palestinian self-rule."

SAVIR: These are just talking points / Joel!

SINGER: Jerusalem.

Tell me, is that why our grandparents were gassed? So we could do this?

(The men stare at each other. No one moves.)

BEILIN: If this is going to work—*if*—Uri is going to have to walk back a great deal more of what's written there. We know that. But the *potential*, Joel. In four months we have gone from not even conceiving of *meeting* these people— *(Pointing to the document)* to that.

Forty years, nothing; now, four *months*, that.

SAVIR: This is not the same old Palestinian bullshit, Joel. I have sat across from these men for *months*, negotiating round after round, and I *know* them. They want this as much as we do.

SINGER: What these men want is unimportant, Uri. What Yasser Arafat will *do* is / all that matters.

SAVIR: Joel. *Listen* to me.

Every negotiating round, my counterpart calls Tunis and speaks *directly* to Arafat. Every point—every concession— these men have made has been signed off on by Arafat.

(Singer stares at Savir and Beilin. They stare back.)

SINGER: Who in the government knows this document exists?

BEILIN: The two of us, and Shimon and Yitzhak.

SINGER *(Shaking his head)*: It's written like mush. The janitor in my law firm would have done a better job. Every sentence in here could be read to mean anything. By either side. It's a fucking time bomb.

BEILIN: So then defuse it.

Yitzhak trusts you, and you alone, to do this.

(Gesturing between Uri and himself) We're not lawyers, Joel. We need your expertise.

(Holding up the DOP) Go through this "mush" and figure out if it can be turned into a real, binding document—or not.

Nothing more can happen between Israel and the PLO unless you tell us it's a go.

Borregaard Estate. The reception room.
Larsen stands before Singer, Savir, Hirschfeld, and Pundak.
Thor and Trond are off to the side. Toril is there as well.

LARSEN *(To Singer)*: And how was your flight? Uneventful I hope?

SINGER: It was fine.

LARSEN: You must be famished.

(Gesturing to her) Toril here has prepared a simple but delicious repast.

SINGER: We're fine.

LARSEN: A drink then!

We shall all have a glass of—

SINGER: We don't need food. And we don't need drinks.

(Finn enters.

He gestures to Larsen: "They're here.")

LARSEN: Ah! Wonderful!

Our other guests have just arrived.

SAVIR *(To Singer, in Hebrew)*: [Joel. Show respect. These men have earned it.]

(Mona enters, bringing in Qurie and Asfour.

Qurie sees the Israelis and stops.)

QURIE: Ah. You are all here.

(To Larsen) Already.

(Then, to the Israelis) Shalom, my friends!

PUNDAK *(Steps forward)*: Salaam alaikum, Abu Ala!

(Singer looks at Pundak. Pundak steps back.)

SAVIR *(Formal)*: Abu Ala, Hassan, it is my great pleasure to introduce you to—

SINGER: They know who I am. And I know who they are. We don't have time for chitchat.

(Staring at Qurie) I have read the text of the joint document created here, and I have come with two hundred questions *about* this document.

QURIE: We reject your questions as we reject your tone.

SINGER: These questions come directly from Yitzhak Rabin. I am here at his personal request. When you are speaking to me, you are speaking to the Prime Minister of Israel.

(No one moves as this sinks in—news to everyone but Savir and Singer.
Qurie gestures to Savir: "Is this true?"
Savir gestures back: "Yes.")

I have until oh-six-hundred hours. We'll need to work through the night.

LARSEN: As you wish.

SINGER: We're wasting time. Let's get started.

(To the professors) Not you two. You've done enough.

HIRSCHFELD: But . . . Uri has assigned us the task of taking minutes.

SINGER: Your task is to do what you're told.

If Uri or I need you, we'll send for you.

(Hirschfeld and Pundak stand rooted as they watch Singer, Savir, and Qurie enter the negotiating room.)

HIRSCHFELD: First we are demoted, now we are exiled?

LARSEN: Yair, I know / this must be difficult.

HIRSCHFELD: I do not accept this! Do you hear me?

LARSEN: / Lower your voice, please.

HIRSCHFELD: They would not even be in that room without us!
We are the ones who started this. *We* took the risks! *This* is what we get? Well fuck them!

(Hirschfeld starts toward the negotiating room.)

LARSEN *(Blocking his way)*: Yair. / Listen to me.

HIRSCHFELD: I will not be discarded / like some piece of trash!

LARSEN: Breathe! Breathe for me!

THIS IS NOT ABOUT YOU!

(Hirschfeld stops struggling.
No one moves.)

PUNDAK: Yair, let's go for a walk.
A little fresh air, yah?

(A moment. Hirschfeld nods.
Mona gestures to Trond: "Go keep an eye on them."
As Hirschfeld and Pundak head for the front door . . .)

LARSEN: Remember, my friends: sometimes we are the pigeon, sometimes we are the statue.

(The two men stare at him. Then they exit with Trond.)

ASFOUR: Comrade Terje, do you know who this man is?
Joel Singer is the man who wrote the military rules of engagement the Zionist army use to crush our people.
We are now in the boat with the enemy himself.

(Asfour enters the negotiating room and closes the door.
Larsen and Mona stare at each other.)

MONA: So, what do you think?
LARSEN: I think this is beyond anything we could have ever imagined.

In the negotiating room.
Singer and Qurie facing each other; Savir and Asfour watching.
Singer holds a folder with paperwork in his hands.

SINGER: Each of these two hundred questions requires a specific, precise answer. When I am satisfied with your answer, we will move on to the next question.
(He looks down at his paperwork then looks up)
If the State of Israel agrees to cede control of Jericho and its surrounding territory, will the proposed Palestinian Authority collect Israeli garbage, or only Palestinian garbage?

(Qurie and Asfour look at each other. Then Qurie turns back to Singer.)

QURIE: This is your question?

SINGER: This is my *first* question.

QURIE: . . . No.

We will not collect Israeli garbage.

SINGER: If the State of Israel agrees to cede control of Jericho and its surrounding territory, will the proposed Palestinian Authority be prepared to send tax collectors into Israeli settlements?

QURIE: Mr. Singer. We did not fly across the world to talk of garbage and taxes.

SINGER: Garbage and taxes is what a government does. If you want us to give you the authority to *be* a government, then this joint document must spell out exactly *how* you will be a government.

(The men stare at each other.)

QURIE: The collecting of Israeli settler taxes will be carried out, and financed, by Israel itself.

(Singer makes a note. He looks back up.)

SINGER: Now, as to education.

Will the proposed Palestinian Authority be in charge of teaching Israeli settler children, and, if so, what specific curricula will you teach them?

MONA *(To us)*: All night they worked. All night, question by question, Singer pushed for clarity.

QURIE: I must speak with Tunis. I require a phone.

(Qurie exits with Trond, as . . .
Singer paces. Savir sits nearby. Asfour sits away from them, watching.
Mona enters with a tray of coffee and coffee cups.)

MONA: We have coffee for everyone.

May I get anyone anything else?

SINGER *(Gesturing off)*: You can get that one out there off the fucking phone.

(To Asfour) How many times is he going to do this? We've already lost an hour and a half.

(To Savir, in Hebrew) [At this rate, we're not going to get through the questions.]

SAVIR *(Hebrew back)*: [Joel. Don't worry. We'll figure it out.]

(As Mona pours coffee . . .)

MONA: Might you be able to extend your visit, Mr. Singer?

SINGER: No. I have to be in Israel tomorrow to brief Yitzhak, then back in DC by tomorrow night.

I told my firm I had to go to my grandmother's funeral in Tel Aviv. At least in *death* the woman's proving useful.

Why are you doing this, you and your husband?

MONA: If you were in our shoes, wouldn't you?

SINGER: No. That's why I'm asking.

MONA: If you have to ask, Mr. Singer, you wouldn't understand my answer.

Outside the room, Trond approaches Larsen.

TROND: Terje, may I have a moment?

LARSEN: Of course, Trond.

TROND: I understand our role here, but I think you should know . . .

(Close, just for him) Whenever Abu Ala goes to use the phone and call Tunis? He does not call Tunis.

LARSEN: Who does he call?

TROND: No one.

He sits, staring at the wall. When enough time for a phone call has passed, he comes back in with "new instructions."

(Larsen stares at him. Then:)

LARSEN: I see.

Thank you.

(As Trond starts to leave . . .)

Trond.
This is just between you and me, yes?
Don't worry Mona with this. I'll take care of it.

Back in the negotiating room.
Ashtrays full. Ties loosened. Nerves frayed.

MONA *(To us)*: Into the morning hours they pushed on.
The scope and complexity of the issues, expanding with each and every question.
SINGER: Will the governing structure overseeing Gaza and Jericho be centralized or *de*centralized?
QURIE: Our governing structure will be as it is in the DOP.
SINGER: It's not *in* the DOP. *That's* why I'm asking.
Centralized or *de*centralized?
ASFOUR: Centralized. With executive and legislative branches.

(Singer stares at Asfour. He stares back.)

SINGER *(To Asfour)*: The phrase "Israeli settlements abutting the city of Jericho" is vague and imprecise. Which settlements, and what are their exact boundaries?
ASFOUR: Settlements and boundaries as per Article Four, page thirty-two, of the working document of the official Washington talks.
SINGER: Show me the language of this document.
ASFOUR: My copy of this document resides here. *(Touches his temple)* Your copy is your business.
MONA *(To us)*: And then the question on which all other points hinged.
SINGER: Are you willing to state herein that you recognize the legitimacy of the State of Israel?

(Silence.
Qurie and Asfour look at each other. Qurie turns back to Singer.)

QURIE: We will agree, in this document, to accept the *existence* of the State of Israel.

SINGER: "Existence" and "legitimacy" are not synonymous.

QURIE: "Existence" is the precise word we have chosen.

SINGER: We *know* we exist. And we know you *see* that we exist. What this document requires is for you to acknowledge the *legitimacy* of our existence.

(No one moves.)

QURIE: Mr. Singer, when *you* are willing to state herein that the Palestine Liberation Organization is the official voice of the Palestinian people—*then* we will revisit your legitimacy.

(The four men stare at each other. Singer and Savir share a look.)

SAVIR *(To Singer, in Hebrew)*: [They've given us enough. For now. Make the offer.]

(Singer turns back to the Palestinians. He closes his folder.)

SINGER: Your answers to my questions were clear and direct. For which you have our thanks and our respect. On behalf of Prime Minister Yitzhak Rabin and the State of Israel, we make this offer: that this back channel will become the official channel.

(Silence. No one moves.)

QURIE: But what of the Washington-sponsored talks?

SINGER: They will continue and no one involved *in* those talks will know that what they are doing is now nothing but a ruse.
If those of us in this room cannot reach an agreement, we do not deserve one.
(Gesturing to Qurie and Savir) You two will negotiate it. *(Gesturing to Asfour)* You and I will write it.
In this room, we four will forge a peace, or there will be no peace.

Larsen and Savir alone.

LARSEN: Uri. My God.

This this this is amazing.

SAVIR: I know.

LARSEN: Mona and I—we had no *inkling* this was even a possibility.

SAVIR: I know.

LARSEN: Did you know that Singer was coming here to present this offer from Rabin?

(Savir stares at him. He says nothing.)

This changes everything. The *possibility* of what can be achieved now!

SAVIR: Terje. Understand: all the chips have just been put on the table. They know now how much we're willing to risk to get this deal. And what a fucking disaster it will be if we don't get it. And we know the exact same thing about them.

When both sides know that both sides *have* to make a deal . . . *that's* when things get dangerous.

Savir is gone.
Mona and Egeland alone.

MONA: Jan, you cannot drop out!

EGELAND: Yes, I can, Mona. And if you have a shred of sense left you will do the same.

I'm off to Kosovo, where I will not be available.

MONA: This process needs you. Look at what has just happened between their two sides!

EGELAND: Yes, exactly: *look.*

I mean, my God, it's one thing for a peace process to have a secret back channel. But now the actual peace process itself is a secret!

The future of two peoples is now being decided—without transparency, without accountability—by a handful of men who have no mandate to do so! If you continue down this path, and the world finds out what you are all doing? There will be riots. Blood will be spilled.

(He turns to go, then turns back)

All political careers end in tragedy, Mona. Don't speed yours up.

Egeland is gone.
Mona faces us.

MONA: The DOP was reworked by Singer, incorporating Abu Ala and Hassan's answers to his questions. It was now a proper, legal document. With it, Singer and Savir returned to Borregaard to meet with the Palestinians.

Later that morning. The reception room. Mona alone.

HIRSCHFELD *(Offstage)*: Mona!
(Racing in, seeing her) Oh, thank God.
Where's Terje?
MONA: He's at a Fafo board meeting.
They called, crack of dawn, demanding he attend. / He couldn't get out of it.
HIRSCHFELD: It's a disaster. Months of work—ruined—by that son of a bitch.
MONA: Yair, what's happened?
HIRSCHFELD: Abu Ala and Hassan started reading the new document—they practically fell off their chairs.
The DOP we made together—it's disappeared.

(As Mona and Hirschfeld continue their conversation, we see Singer and Savir face-off with Asfour and Qurie; Pundak is to the side. They all hold copies of the new draft of the DOP in their hands.)

QURIE: What is this page?! And *this*?!
HIRSCHFELD: What Singer has brought, it's almost a complete rewrite.

QURIE: Every word, a fiction!

HIRSCHFELD: He took out that we agree to give them Jericho. And he put *in* that *they* agree to everything we have asked for.

SAVIR: What is in there is what you said to us in response to our two hundred questions!

QURIE: Saying and writing are not the same—and you know this!

HIRSCHFELD: Abu Ala is screaming. Hassan is ballistic.

ASFOUR: You will not grind your boot into our throat!

HIRSCHFELD: You have to fix this.

(Cutting her off before she can speak) No!

Mona, you are part of this now. Go. In.

Inside the negotiating room.

As one, the men turn and see Mona standing there in the room, Hirschfeld behind her.

They stare at her—then whirl back on each other.

ASFOUR: This is not a "joint approach," this is an Israeli occupation! You have no right to tell us how *our* army will respond to *our* people!

SINGER: We are not going one step further until you agree—as written there—that the violence ceases when you are in charge.

ASFOUR: We are in Tunis. Those who are occupied began the Intifada. It is theirs to end when they see fit!

SINGER: Then why the fuck are we talking to you?

SAVIR: Joel, *I* am negotiating, yes? / Then let me negotiate.

QURIE: Uri, why do you refuse to recognize the historic compromises we have already made?

SAVIR: *You* have made? Abu Ala, we are giving you *land*. We are shrinking the size of our country!

QURIE: This is land not for you to give, but to give back!

SAVIR: This is land you fucking *lost* because you invaded *us*—and we kicked your fucking ass!

QURIE: Where—in this—where is Jerusalem?

SINGER: You put Jerusalem back on the table and everything is over.

QURIE *(To Savir)*: Don't you see? You go on like this, you will never stop being the occupier—and we will never stop fighting you!

SINGER: Your fighting is killing your own children.

ASFOUR: Our fighting has forced you to stand in this room and deal with us!

QURIE *(To Savir)*: My friend, listen to me! Together / we can fix this.

SINGER: He. Works. For. ME!

SAVIR: Let us be fucking clear, Joel. You are here for Yitzhak, / I am here for Shimon—equals, whether you like it or not.

SINGER: This is / when you want to have this conversation? Really? Now?

ASFOUR *(To Singer, in Arabic)*: / [We will bury you! We will bury you!]

QURIE *(To Savir, pointing at Singer)*: Poison! This one pours poison, in all our ears!

MAN'S VOICE *(Over them, offstage)*: Ah-lo?

(All freeze—statues, mid-word and action.)

(Offstage) Ah-*lo*-ho?

(Gestures fly around the room: "Who is that?" "What do we do?" "Where can we hide?"
A German Husband and Wife enter the room, suitcases in hand.)

HUSBAND: Ah! Here you are.
(Taking out a piece of paper) We are looking for . . . Toril?

(Mona and the roomful of men stare at the couple. They stare back.)

MONA *(As Toril)*: Yah, I am Toril.
(Gesturing to Singer) This is Finn, my husband.

SINGER *(Beat. Then)*: Yah.

HUSBAND: We know we are twenty-three minutes early, but we would like to check in now.

MONA: Ah.

Yah.

Terrible mix-up. There are no rooms.

HUSBAND: What are you talking about? We have a reservation.

MONA: We are remodeling.

(Gesturing to the other men) This is our crew.

(The other men in the room mumble "Ah-lo"s with their eyes downcast.)

HUSBAND *(To Wife, in German)*: [She says there are no rooms.]
WIFE *(In German)*: [But we have a reservation!]
HUSBAND *(In German)*: [That's what I told her.]
WIFE *(In German)*: [Hans! This is where we stay. Fix this.]
HUSBAND *(To Mona)*: This is outrageous! We had this reservation for nine months and three days!
MONA: We will refund, and get you better rooms, very close by.
HUSBAND: We are not leaving!
MONA: Please, sir, if you will step out / I will be right with you.
HUSBAND: We will call the media! Do you hear me? We will tell the local constabulary—
MONA *(In German)*: [SHUT YOUR MOUTH.]
[Go outside and wait for me or your safety cannot be guaranteed.]

(Silence. The couple stares at her, mouths open. Then:)

HUSBAND: Take your time.

(They scoot out of the room.
The men stare at Mona.)

SAVIR: What a / woman. I mean, what a woman!
QURIE: This is my daughter! My daughter!
MONA: Stop it. Stop it. We don't have time.
(To all of them) Listen to me.
You have fought each other—killed each other—for fifty years. Your mothers and daughters and sons have died, and nothing has changed.
The world has washed its hands of this conflict, because they do not believe you *can* change.
No one else is coming to help you. So it is up to you.
Stay in this room and find a way forward.

(She exits.
The men are alone. Staring at each other.
Singer picks up a copy of the DOP.)

SINGER: I'm willing to start at the top. Go through. See what we
can see.

(Asfour stares at Singer. Then:)

ASFOUR: As are we.

Outside the room, Mona paces, charged with energy. Larsen races in—
out of breath.

LARSEN *(Gasping)*: Mona!
    I got here as soon as I could.
MONA *(Gasping as well)*: Terje, they are in there, at the table, push-
    ing on.
LARSEN: Are they close to a deal?
MONA: Yes. Both sides are almost there.
    Nothing is going to stop this!
LARSEN: Nothing!

Holst appears.

HOLST: The Israelis are pulling out.
LARSEN AND MONA: What?!

Oslo. The Foreign Ministry.
Holst and Marianne; Mona and Larsen.

HOLST: They want to close the Channel—now.
LARSEN: But, Johan Jorgen, the progress they just made—it was
    incredible!
MARIANNE: Too incredible. They don't believe it's possible the
    PLO has made these latest concessions.

LARSEN: I'm sorry, you are here *why* again, Marianne?

HOLST: She's a guest, Terje. Here to advise. Like yourself.

MONA: What are the Israelis afraid of—specifically?

HOLST: That Arafat is setting them up. The Channel—all of it— is simply an elaborate trap to bring down the Israeli Government.

MARIANNE: If we were in the Israelis' shoes, wouldn't we be paranoid? This is Yasser Arafat we're talking about. I know we're neutral but—please.

MONA: If we need to convince the Israelis, let's go to Arafat and test him one more time.

MARIANNE: That's a terrible idea. We've stuck our necks out on this far enough.

LARSEN: "We"? I'm sorry, who is this / "we," Marianne?

MARIANNE: I have just as much right to be here as you, Terje.

LARSEN: Or at Fafo, where you are paid to do a job I hired you to do.

MARIANNE: Now would that be the institute you have abandoned while you chase personal glory? You are an interloper Terje, / who will do anything to rise above your station.

LARSEN: You know, Marianne, *humility* is the virtue that tightens the skin.

(Shaking the skin under his neck) You should look into it!

MONA: ENOUGH!

(Beat. All three stare at Mona.)

Johan Jorgen, the risks are real but they don't outweigh the opportunity.

Let's go to Tunis. We'll stand in front of Arafat, *read* him the document, and *see* if he truly knows what this is.

Beilin and Savir appear.

BEILIN: You can't be serious.

MONA *(To us)*: Jerusalem. The Foreign Ministry.

(Beilin and Savir across from Holst, Mona, and Larsen.)

LARSEN: I am *beyond* serious!

And this is the best part. Halfway through the presentation, Arafat slaps the table, and wags his finger.

(As Arafat) "There must be kissing points!"

I say, "Mr. Chairman, do you mean checkpoints?"

(As Arafat) "No, Larsen!"

(Forefingers "kissing" each other) "Kissing points. Kiss, kiss, kiss."

SAVIR: So our territorial boundaries should abut?

MONA: Yes, that's what we *think* he meant.

LARSEN: *Then,* as Johan Jorgen is reading him the draft document, he starts bouncing up and down on his seat, yelling:

(As Arafat) "I am not Nelson Mandela! I am not Nelson Mandela!"

SAVIR: But what does Arafat say about the document? Does he agree with what's in it or not?

HOLST: Not only did he agree with it, he had complete command of the details. He quoted entire sections along with me. Frankly, I'm amazed.

SAVIR *(To Beilin)*: Good! All right! See? We have to push on!

BEILIN: We all want this deal. But Arafat has *always* played the wild card, right at the / last moment.

SAVIR: Yossi, I know it's a huge fucking risk, but it's now or never!

BEILIN: We don't know that!

SAVIR: Come on, Yossi! You know I'm right!

BEILIN: Uri, you are being reckless! / Focus on our objective!

SAVIR: Don't fucking tell me what I am being!

LARSEN: My friends! Let us—

SAVIR: MIND YOUR BUSINESS!

(Then) Yossi.

This is what we have waited for our entire lives.

BEILIN: Uri. It's not our decision to make.

Shimon Peres, seventy, Foreign Minister of the State of Israel, draped in the most exquisite of suits, appears.

PERES *(To us)*: This reminds me of a story.

You'll find it very interesting.

When I was a young man, I told my mother that my dearest wish was to become a fighter pilot. She said she would allow it—on one condition. That I fly very slowly and very close to the ground.

I replied, "But, Mother, for a pilot to be safe, he must fly very fast and very high."

(To Larsen) I adore your shoes.

LARSEN: Thank you.

PERES: Do you have them stretched, or break them in yourself?

LARSEN: Stretched, without question. This way / they are prepared to be shaped by the foot.

PERES: Yes, the leather: far more supple in the end.

BEILIN: Shimon, if we could, the PLO? Arafat?

PERES: What we must not do is allow the details to obscure the bigger picture. If this deal does not happen, the PLO will be so hollowed out, so bereft of victories, it may well cease to exist. This we cannot allow. For Israel *needs* the PLO to exist.

(Off shocked faces) Well I don't love them either, but when I look at the alternatives, I become very romantic.

(To Mona) Speaking of this, do you have plans for dinner?

(To them all) Arafat is tricky, but he is a man. And a man aches for one thing above all. His home.

(To Savir) Tell your counterpart to tell Arafat that if he makes this deal with us, I will allow him and the rest of the PLO leadership to return to Gaza.

BEILIN: Shimon. The PLO—*Arafat*—In Gaza?

PERES: If we are to be bold, it must be now.

(To them all) Get them all back to Oslo, for one last round.

And from now on we tell the Americans nothing.

HOLST: But, Shimon—

Nothing?

PERES: The Americans cannot stand it when others take the lead. I was *this* close to making peace with King Hussein and the Jordanians—until the Americans got wind and scuttled it. This, they will not scuttle.

MONA: But the Americans could ask, directly, at any moment. Terje and I know this firsthand.

PERES: If they ask—any of us—we say the Channel is closed.

HOLST: You . . . you mean, flat-out lie?

PERES: Well, what is a lie but a dream that could come true? Fast and high, my friends: it is the only way.

Warplanes. Tank fire.

MONA *(To us)*: Twenty-four July. Israel launches a full-on assault against Hezbollah in southern Lebanon. Two hundred thousand refugees stream toward Beirut. Casualties in the hundreds. Reprisal rockets kill Israeli civilians.

The crowd of Palestinian Citizens again fills the stage.

(To us) Meanwhile, in Tunis, the PLO's telephone lines are cut off due to unpaid bills. Salaries are frozen.

PALESTINIAN CITIZENS *(In Arabic)*: [Let us work!]

MONA *(To us)*: The PLO is unable to pay welfare to fifty thousand families in the Occupied Territories, who have no other income.

PALESTINIAN CITIZENS *(In Arabic)*: [Let us work!]

MONA *(To us)*: And none of this is mentioned—not a word, by either side—as they push on. In this room, in this castle, for one last round.

A frayed Singer, Savir, Qurie, and Asfour in the negotiating room.

SAVIR: End of Article Eight. The sentence: "Israel will continue to carry all responsibilities," must be followed by the words: "for defending against external threats or terrorist threats."

QURIE: We will accept "external threats," but not "terrorist threats."

SAVIR: Agreed.

QURIE: The long-standing UN Resolutions 242 and 338 criticizing the Israeli occupation *must* be included in this document.

SAVIR: That we categorically reject. But if you are willing to postpone discussion on the future of Israeli settlements—

QURIE: No. We will not.

But.

The Right of Return for those displaced in the '67 War . . .
This we agree to postpone to a later date.

SAVIR: And if you are willing to accept our control of border
security . . . We will withdraw all our forces from Gaza *and*
Jericho at the same time.

QURIE: The City of Jerusalem will be the capital for both—

SAVIR AND SINGER: NO.

Borregaard Estate. The drawing room. Very late.
Thor is drunk, standing before an equally soused Singer and Savir, and
Qurie and Asfour, and Hirschfeld—while Pundak slumps in a chair,
passed out. As Larsen refills their whiskey glasses . . .

THOR: Abu Ala, I am telling you what I believe: you people drive
me crazy.

(Pointing between the Israelis and Palestinians) There is no
difference between you!

(Over their laughter) Now, if you want to talk about Norwegians
and *Swedes*, then we are talking about differences.

SINGER *(Rising)*: I'll tell you what drives *me* crazy.

If I hear one more Israeli say Israel is part of the "West," I'm
going to punch them. All those fuckers in Tel Aviv, acting
like they live in California. Like all they have to worry about
is their tans and their swimming pools. Yeah, the West are
our allies, but we are not *them*.

ASFOUR: At least you *have* allies, comrade. What we have is lip
service.

(Cutting them all off before they can speak) Egyptians, Jordanians,
Kuwaitis, Iranians, Saudis—their governments beat their
breasts about the "Plight of the Palestinians," but they do
not give a fuck about the Palestinians. Our cause is an opiate
they inject into the proletariat masses so they will not turn
their anger on their own decadent capitalist masters!

SAVIR *(Pretend "aside")*: Abu Ala, I don't want to alarm you, but
I think that one might be a communist.

QURIE *("Aside" back to him)*: No, he is a Swedish Norwegian Californian from Tel Aviv. *They* are far worse.

SINGER *(Rolling on)*: *Our* people are the worst! Too fucking chickenshit to own up to who we are. "Oh, please, don't blame us. We didn't do anything." Bullshit. We fought wars, and we won wars, and the territory and the consequences are *ours!*

LARSEN: So you are Sparta and not Athens, Joel?

SAVIR: And there goes Terje, with his charm and his refilling.

HIRSCHFELD: Thank God for his refilling!

PUNDAK: Terje, who do you refill the most? Come on, tell us!

LARSEN: My friends, discretion forbids me from revealing such a thing.

(He points out Savir; all but Savir roar in delight.)

PUNDAK: Ha! It's so true!

SAVIR: You're quite the trickster, Terje.

Tell me, does anyone ever trick you?

(Turning to Qurie) This one likes to run his mouth, doesn't he, Abu Ala?

QURIE: You are right, Uri. This one is talk and talk and nothing else.

LARSEN: Well how fortunate that we are here *to* talk, yes?

SAVIR: Yes, *we* are here to talk, but why are *you* here, Terje?

LARSEN: To be of service, of course, to you all.

SAVIR: Service? Really?

(Leaning in) We *see* you, Terje. Don't think we do not.

HIRSCHFELD: Come on! Terje is here for all of us.

SAVIR *(Eyes on Larsen)*: Shut up, Yair.

LARSEN *(Beat. Then)*: My friends, I know we are frayed, but we are all in this together.

SAVIR: No, *we* are in this; *you* are watching. So don't tell us how we should think or act.

QURIE: Who does he think he is, Uri? Telling us what to do. This underwear merchant posing as a diplomat.

Back home, we would chop him in half.

SAVIR: Yes, let us do that, Abu Ala, and we will give the lower half to Mona.

(Larsen and Savir stare at each other. No one moves.)

LARSEN: I will not stand here and be your punching bag.

SAVIR: You will stand here and do whatever we want, because that's your job.
(To the room) Okay. Enough with him. Now, look, my "Kissinger" is good, right? Right?
But I do *this* one even better.
(To Qurie and Asfour) With respect, my friends.
(A dramatic pause as he "gets into character"; then, to them all, as Arafat:)
"Ah, welcome to Tunis. I am so honored to have you as my guests."

*(Shock and delight from the others—except for Larsen.
"Arafat" gestures to Ahmed Qurie.)*

"This is my esteemed Finance Minister.
Tell us, Abu Ala, how goes the peacemaking?"

QURIE: Ah, Mr. Chairman, these Israelis, they are wily, but we are pinning them down.

SAVIR: "I am so pleased. Now, tell me of the other Grandfather. Is he as charming and beautiful as me?"

HIRSCHFELD: Uri, it's a little uncanny, / I have to say.

PUNDAK: Go on, go on! Do some more!

SAVIR *(Gesturing to Larsen)*: "I see you there, in the back. Don't be shy. Here, we are all friends, yes?"
"Ah, look at him: he is afraid of me!"

(Larsen steps forward. Then, in the gravely voice of Yitzhak Rabin:)

LARSEN *(As Rabin)*: "On the contrary, Mr. Chairman, it is you who should be afraid of me."

(The room explodes with giddiness.)

SAVIR: "Ah, Prime Minster Rabin! How good of you to join us, Your Excellency."

SINGER: Okay, this is fucking weird.

SAVIR *(Eyes on Larsen)*: "This is a momentous meeting: we Grand-fathers, face-to-face."

LARSEN *(Staring back)*: "Enemy-to-enemy."

SAVIR: "How true.

So. What do you think of me?"

LARSEN: "That you look like a man I could snap in half."

(The room is silent—the men glued to their chairs as "Arafat" and "Rabin" face-off.)

SAVIR: "Tell me, Your Excellency, why should I believe you could do that, when you won't even let your soldiers use real bullets on my people as they fight you in Gaza?"

LARSEN: "But all I need is *one* bullet, Mr. Chairman. Just for you. You make all the peace you want. But one day, I will come for you."

HIRSCHFELD *(Rising)*: Okay. Okay.

(Hirschfeld "draws" a line on the floor between Savir and Larsen.)

Red line. Yah? *Red. Line.*

(Beat. Savir slowly, deliberately, walks over the "line." He's face-to-face with Larsen.)

SAVIR: "You've dreamed of this moment, haven't you, Yitzhak? To have me, inches from you. *Me.* The One Himself. What do you want to do? What do you *dare* do?"

(Larsen lunges—gripping Savir's lapels—a spell broken—the men rise to their feet.
Everyone is frozen, a collective breath held.
Larsen slides his hands down to Savir's shoulders, then slowly leans in and kisses him on one cheek, then the other.
Larsen walks through the men, and out the door.
No one else moves.
Then—
A phone rings.)

MONA *(To us)*: One week later. Our flat in Oslo. Early Sunday morning.

(Larsen picks up the phone as Beilin appears.)

LARSEN: Al-lo?

BEILIN *(Outward)*: Terje, this is the Son, calling with a message from the Father.

LARSEN: Of course. What does he—

BEILIN: Terje. The Father says you need to assemble your team and fly tomorrow, in secret, to Stockholm, Sweden. Tomorrow night the Father will be attending a state dinner there. After the dinner, the Father will meet your team at the royal guesthouse, and then he will make it.

LARSEN: Sorry, ah, make what?

BEILIN: Peace. With Those Across the Sea.

We are going to finish it, Terje, tomorrow night.

Stockholm. The next night.
The Swedish royal guesthouse for visiting dignitaries.
The guesthouse's Swedish Hostess stares at Mona and Larsen.

SWEDISH HOSTESS: How long will you be with Mr. Peres tonight?

MONA: As long as Mr. Peres wishes.

SWEDISH HOSTESS: And why are you here to see Mr. Peres?

MONA: Mr. Peres, I'm sure, would like to answer that himself.

(The Hostess stares at Mona and Larsen. They smile. She does not. They wait.)

LARSEN: Perhaps a bit of late supper? Could that be arranged?

SWEDISH HOSTESS: The kitchen is closed.

(They wait.
Shimon Peres enters in a tuxedo.)

Ah, Mr. Foreign Minister. How was your function?

PERES: Long.

SWEDISH HOSTESS: May I get you something from the kitchen?

PERES: No, thank you.

SWEDISH HOSTESS: This couple is not on the official list for the guesthouse.

PERES: Good.

You may leave us.

(She hesitates, stares at Larsen and Mona, then does so.)

Holst is still at the reception, but he is coming.

Let us get started.

(Larsen and Mona look at each other.)

LARSEN: But, ah—

(Looking around) Where are the Palestinians?

PERES: The Palestinians are not coming.

(Larsen gestures to Mona: "What??!!"

She gestures back: "Don't.")

LARSEN: Ah. Shimon. Usually, as I know you know, when there are negotiations between two parties, there *are* two parties.

PERES: We are doing this on the phone.

You will ring Tunis, tell them I am calling, and have them put Arafat on the line.

MONA: Is the PLO leadership expecting your call?

PERES: The PLO leadership has never spoken to the Israeli leadership. Ever.

But the Chairman and I are the only ones who can make the necessary and painful final compromises. Since he and I can have no contact—of any kind—we will use Johan Jorgen as our intermediary.

Here is the latest draft of the DOP, with Singer's markings.

Now, dial Tunis and find Arafat.

The night is not young, my friends, and we have a long way to go.

(He exits.)

LARSEN: Seriously? "Dial Tunis"? Like there's only one phone number there? This is Arafat! He is *unreachable* by phone.

MONA: Where is Abu Ala?

LARSEN: I don't know.

MONA: Is he in Tunis?

LARSEN: I don't know!

(Mona gets paperwork and goes to the phone.)

What are you doing?

MONA *(To Larsen)*: We're going to call every possible number where Abu Ala could be staying. *He* will know how to get to Arafat.

(As Thor enters . . .)

THOR: Terje, the perimeter is secure.

LARSEN: Thank you, Thor.

(As Thor exits, Trond enters . . .)

TROND: Terje, Minister Holst is on his way.

LARSEN: Excellent, Trond.

MONA *(To us)*: Two hours went by. We kept calling. But we could not reach Abu Ala.

Later. Holst is with them now—dressed in a tuxedo, as he paces.

HOLST: Christ, it's almost midnight. We're running out of time.

MONA: We'll find him.

We *will*, Johan Jorgen.

HOLST: Where's Shimon?

MONA: He said to wake him when we got Arafat on the line, but not before.

LARSEN: We need more copies of the new DOP.

OSLO

105

(The Hostess enters.)

SWEDISH HOSTESS: Mr. Peres has retired for the evening so this office is closed.

MONA: Mr. Peres will be joining us again in a few moments.

May we use your copy machine?

SWEDISH HOSTESS: The copy machine is closed.

(As she pivots, and exits . . .
Qurie, on the phone, facing outward.)

QURIE: Hello? Can you hear me?

LARSEN: Oh, thank God.

QURIE: Can you *hear* me? This / connection is rubbish.

LARSEN: Yes, yes. Puntoffle. Listen to me.

I am calling for the Father. He is here, *with* me. He wishes to speak to your Grandfather. Person to person. Through this phone. Through an intermediary.

To finish it. Now. Tonight.

(Silence. Qurie digests this.)

Do you understand what / I am saying?

QURIE: Yes.

I do.

Yes.

(Silence. Then:)

I will call you back.

LARSEN: No! Puntoffle we don't have time for—

QURIE: Larsen. I will call you back.

(And he's gone. Larsen turns to Holst and Mona.)

MONA *(To us)*: An hour. Then another.

(Trond enters.)

TROND: Mona, there's a problem.

> I went to make copies of the DOP. No one saw me. But it's stuck in the copy machine and I can't get it out.

MONA: Then ask her for help.

TROND: But she said we couldn't use the machine.

MONA: Trond, do you have your gun?

TROND: Yes.

> *(She gestures to him: "Then use it!"*
> *As he turns and exits . . .*
> *Qurie reappears, speaking outward.)*

QURIE: Larsen, I am here.

LARSEN: Puntoffle! Thank God.

> *(Larsen gestures to Mona and Holst: "It's him! Get on the phone now!"*
> *Mona and Holst are on the phone as well now, facing outward, phones gripped.)*

QURIE: I am with the Grandfather.

LARSEN: Excellent.

QURIE: And with the entire ruling council.

LARSEN: Puntoffle . . . the entire . . . they are *all* with you?

QURIE: Here, around a table, yes.

> He has just informed them of our Channel and what is to now transpire.

LARSEN: And and the news—my God—how are they taking it?

QURIE: Let us move on.

> The Grandfather's English is not as he wishes. Therefore he asks that I speak for and to him.

LARSEN: I understand. I'm sure that won't—

QURIE: And I ask that *you* are the one I speak to.

> *(Larsen looks at Holst and Mona who stand still, phones to their ears.)*

LARSEN *(To Qurie)*: But, ah, ah the intermediary, it is to be—I am sure you know whom I am speaking of, his high *official* capacity in *my* country.

QURIE: You are speaking of the one who is the Lord Over Your Wife.

LARSEN: Well. That's not. The code *I* would choose, but—

QURIE: Is the Lord Over Your Wife listening?

(Larsen looks to Holst, who gestures "no.")

LARSEN: Yes.

QURIE: Then the Lord knows the respect that I hold the Lord in. And he will understand that where I am from, what men begin together, men must finish together.

(Qurie waits for an answer.
Holst stares at Larsen. He looks at Mona. Then:)

HOLST: I'll get Shimon.

(He exits.
Larsen and Qurie do not move. They wait. And wait.)

QURIE: Are you still there?

LARSEN: Yes.

(They do not move. They wait.)

QURIE: Are you / still there?

LARSEN: Yes, I *am*. Puntoffle. Trust me.

(Peres and Holst enter.)

HOLST *(To Peres)*: It is a total breach of protocol. If you are uneasy with this in anyway, I will instruct Arafat's intermediary—

PERES: I understand. And it is. But, Johan Jorgen, I think we must acknowledge that now we are all very far beyond the bounds of protocol.

(Peres puts his hand out. Beat. Holst puts the phone in Peres's hand.)

J.T. ROGERS

108

(To Larsen) Let us begin.

(Larsen faces outward, flanked on each side by the outward-looking Peres and Qurie. Mona speaks to us.)

MONA: Seven hours. Terje, the go-between for both sides.

LARSEN *(As if to Peres)*: The Grandfather says he cannot accept that.

MONA: The final intransigents, on the table.

LARSEN *(As if to Qurie)*: The Father says he is going to bed; call him when you change your mind.

MONA: Argue. Hang up. Call back. Push on.

QURIE: We will accept that their forces be in charge of border security, but *our* forces must have joint control of all checkpoints.

PERES: Tell him our checkpoints, our soldiers; we will not cede this point.

QURIE: Tell him the Grandfather says, then we will burn this document and wage war upon you until the last days of time. But also that we are open to a counter proposal.

MONA: Nerves frayed. Voices hoarse. But, slowly:

PERES: We will accept . . . that the Palestine Liberation Organization is the official voice of the Palestinian People.

MONA: One after another.

QURIE: We will accept . . . the *legitimacy* of the State of Israel.

MONA: Hour by hour.

QURIE: Agreed.

MONA: Point by point.

PERES: Agreed.

MONA: Except:

PERES: Jerusalem. Will remain solely the capital of Israel.

QURIE: No!

PERES: Non-negotiable!

(Silence. No one moves.)

QURIE: Larsen. Tell him. This is not the bluffing.

(Silence. All wait.

Larsen lowers his phone, leans in, and starts whispering in Peres's ear.

Mona and Holst are gesturing wildly to Larsen: "What are you doing?!?"

Peres stands still, listening. Larsen finishes. He pulls back.

No one moves. Then:)

PERES: In the name of . . . constructive ambiguity . . . we will accept that in the *final* stage of *further* negotiations, the future of Jerusalem will be addressed.

(Silence. Peres, Qurie, and Larsen stare outward.)

QURIE: We accept this document.
PERES: As do we.

(No one moves. No one can believe it.)

LARSEN: Abu Ala . . . What is that sound?
QURIE *(Beat. Then)*: They are crying.
 All of them.
 They did not think they would live to see this day.

Washington, DC. The White House. Reception room.
A great murmur of voices offstage. Larsen is busy with the seating arrangements for the post-ceremony reception. Thor and Trond assist him.

MONA *(To us)*: 13 September 1993. Washington, DC. The White House.

(The American Diplomat enters.)

AMERICAN DIPLOMAT: Terje! *(Still mispronouncing his name "TUR-juh")* Good to see you.
LARSEN: Ah, yes. It's been so long.
AMERICAN DIPLOMAT: That's quite a press corps out there.

LARSEN: They are saying it is unprecedented. From every corner of the world.

AMERICAN DIPLOMAT: Appears we have you to blame for that. Hope nothing goes wrong. That'd be on you, wouldn't it?

LARSEN: Ha. Yes. That's—

(The doors fly open and Qurie and Savir burst through, mid-argument.)

QURIE *(Simultaneously)*: It cannot be changed, it will not be changed, it is as it is, and that is final!

Uri, it is not my decision. And I cannot change it!

SAVIR *(Simultaneously)*: How can you possibly think we would agree to this? Now? / An hour before the fucking thing is unveiled to the world?

LARSEN *(To the men)*: My friends, my friends! Take this somewhere else—please!

(As Mona enters . . .)

QURIE: Mona, you must see the rightness of our cause and help my people.

SAVIR *(To Mona)*: Tell him they cannot alter the treaty *sixty minutes* before we are signing in front of the world.

QURIE: You are making peace with *us,* not some pretend foe you can name as you wish!

MONA: What is—Abu Ala—what is going on?

SAVIR: I'll fucking tell you.

(Pointing at Qurie) They have changed—throughout the document—every time it says "Palestine" to read "PLO."

QURIE: For that is who we are!

SAVIR: Abu Ala, it cannot happen!

Can you not understand what the word "PLO" means to us? What our enemies back home, the ones who want to tear this treaty up, how they will use this to—

Listen to me! Peres and Rabin are leaving. They are packing their bags and leaving—*right now.*

I am not bluffing.

Do you understand?

QURIE: And I, too, Uri.

The Chairman will sign as he requests, or he will leave. Now.

(Silence. No one moves.)

AMERICAN DIPLOMAT: Well, this is a pickle.

(The rest of the room turns and looks at him.)

Clearly this is a complex issue, and had we more time, it could be addressed in a gradual manner.

QURIE: Yes, but it cannot be denied that—

AMERICAN DIPLOMAT: I'm. Still. Talking.

(Beat. Then back to them all) But we don't. Have the time.

Because people are waiting.

So.

Here's what's gonna happen.

(To Savir) You'll accept the word "PLO" and sign the document. If your leadership has any problems with that, they can speak to Warren Christopher.

(To Qurie) Tell *your* leadership, no more changes.

(To them all) See you out there.

And congratulations.

(And he is out the door—gone.
Beat. Then . . .)

MONA: I think we should all get ready.

(Mumbles of "yes," "of course."
Savir and Qurie exit.)

LARSEN *(Stopping her)*: Darling, I have been working through the seating chart for dinner after, but I don't have our seating for the ceremony.

MONA: Terje, there are no seats for us at the ceremony.

LARSEN: What do you mean?

Darling.

I know we are not going to be standing up there on the dais, but—

MONA: We can stand in the back and watch.

(He stares at her.)

LARSEN: "In the back"?
   Are you.
   Mona.
   How?
MONA: Terje. It's not about you.

(Larsen stares at her. She stares back.
He turns, and exits.
For a moment, Mona is alone onstage.
Then the Company fills the space.
As one, they turn upstage, backs to us as they, and we, watch
footage from the Rose Garden ceremony of September 13, 1993—
Prime Minister Yitzhak Rabin and Chairman Yasser Arafat
shaking hands; President Bill Clinton standing between them—as
we hear the gravely voice of Rabin:)

VOICE OF RABIN: "Let me say to you, the Palestinians—we are destined to live together on the same soil in the same land. We, the soldiers who have returned from battles stained with blood; we, who have seen our relatives and friends killed before our eyes; we, who have attended the funerals and cannot look into the eyes of their parents; we, who have come from a land where parents bury their children; we, who have fought against you, the Palestinians; we say to you today, in a loud and clear voice—enough of blood and tears. Enough!"

(No one moves. Then, as one, the Company turns around to face us.)

MONA: January 1994.
HOLST: Four months after the Rose Garden signing, Johan Jorgen Holst dies of a heart attack.

BEILIN: One month later, an Israeli settler kills twenty-nine Palestinians as they pray at the Cave of the Patriarchs in Hebron.

SAVIR: Tel Aviv. November 1995.

SINGER: During a demonstration in support of the Oslo Accords, Prime Minister Yitzhak Rabin is assassinated by an Israeli extremist who opposes them.

QURIE: February 1996.

On a bus in Jerusalem, a Palestinian suicide bomber detonates himself, killing twenty-six Israelis.

ASFOUR: And in the hallway of his apartment building in Gaza, Hassan Asfour is beaten almost to death. His attackers are never found. He retires from public life.

MONA: September 2000.

SINGER: Seven years to the month after the Accords were signed, violence reerupts in the Occupied Territories.

BEILIN: The Second Intifada begins.

QURIE: Ahmed Qurie becomes Prime Minister of the Palestinian Authority. Two years later the PLO is defeated at the ballot box by Hamas. He retires from public life.

MARIANNE: November 2004.

Marianne Heiberg dies of a heart attack.

PERES: And at the same time, in a hospital in a suburb of Paris, His Excellency, Chairman Yasser Arafat dies.

PUNDAK: April 2014.

Ron Pundak dies of cancer.

PERES: September 2016.

Shimon Peres, the last surviving founder of the State of Israel, dies.

SINGER: Joel Singer lives on.

BEILIN: Yossi Beilin lives on.

SAVIR: To this day, Uri Savir and Ahmed Qurie, and their daughters, have never been out of touch.

(Mona and Larsen are alone onstage.)

LARSEN *(Gesturing to us)*: Mona, tell them.

Without the Oslo Channel, there would be no Palestinian Authority. We—all of us, together—we made the eventuality of a Palestinian State accepted by the world. We helped the Israelis safeguard their future.

MONA: Terje.

LARSEN: Without Oslo there would have been no peace between Israel and Jordan. No withdrawal of Israeli forces from Lebanon. Of Israeli forces from Gaza. Of—

MONA: Terje!
I am trying. But, even now, I am struggling. To know if what we did—*how* we did—was right.

(They stare at each other.)

LARSEN: Then *I* will tell them.

(Larsen turns to us.
Slowly, he advances toward us as he speaks.)

We created a *process*.
Seeing all this, is that not clear?
A model—that *can* be used again—to bring implacable enemies together, to find a way forward. Together.

(He stands still, taking us all in.)

My friends, do not look at where we *are*; look behind you.
(He points behind) There! *See* how far we have come!
If we have come *this* far, through blood, through fear—hatred—how much *further* can we yet go?
(Points ahead) There! On the horizon. The Possibility.
Do you see it?
Do you?

(He waits. He stares at us.)

Good.

END OF PLAY

ACKNOWLEDGMENTS

First and foremost, my thanks to Bartlett Sher and André Bishop.

As I write in the introduction herein, Bart set up the initial meeting that started me down the path to this play. From inception to opening night, he has been my partner on this project. Bart's endless, incisive questions pushed me to cut, clarify, and improve; his staging of the play is a thing of rigorous beauty.

André gave *Oslo* a slot in the Lincoln Center Theater season before I had written a word. He then committed the theater's resources to a series of workshops, giving Bart and me a laboratory to work on both the script and its staging. What more could a playwright ask for?

This play would not exist without them, and I dedicate it to them.

When I had researched endlessly but not yet put pen to paper, New Dramatists and the Weston Playhouse sent me off to seclusion in Vermont. The time and space there—along with the encouragement of fellow secluded playwrights Erin Courtney and Clarence Coo—unlocked the play, and I was able to begin. Bless them all.

Early in the writing of *Oslo*, the PlayPenn New Play Development Conference in Philadelphia, led by Paul Meshejian, gave me space and time to work. With the assistance of director Tyne Rafaeli and our company of actors, I was able to finish a first, great beast of a draft. Board member Victor F. Keen then provided space for Tyne, the actors, and me to reconvene and continue working on the play. All involved have my immense gratitude.

My thanks to the Doris Duke Charitable Foundation. Through their Theatre Commissioning and Production Initiative, they gave me money to pay my bills. Their timing and generosity were a godsend.

The list of actors in New York City and Philadelphia who read this play for me as I wrote it (and wrote it and wrote it) would stretch on for pages, so let me say here collectively what I've said to each of them in person: thank you from the bottom of my heart.

I cannot sing the praises enough of the cast, designers, production team, and crew that brought *Oslo* to life at Lincoln Center Theater. Has any playwright ever had such a team of collaborators? Daily, they awed, thrilled, and inspired me.

Finally, my ongoing gratitude to three people who continue to shape my life:

Rebecca Ashley, my beloved partner in all things, on whose shrewd notes and wise counsel I daily rely. Her influence on this author's work and life can't be overstated.

John Buzzetti, my first and only theater agent, who has championed me for my entire career. I am blessed—truly—to have him in my corner, and as my friend.

My father, Marvin L. Rogers, who passed on to me his love of politics and history, and his joy of a good joke. The best one in this play was told to me by him. Thanks, Dad.

J. T. ROGERS's plays include *Oslo* (Lincoln Center Theater); *Blood and Gifts* (National Theatre, London; Lincoln Center Theater); *The Overwhelming* (National Theatre, followed by UK tour with Out of Joint; Roundabout Theatre); *White People* (Off-Broadway with Starry Night Entertainment); and *Madagascar* (Theatre503, London; Melbourne Theatre Company). He was nominated for an Olivier Award as one of the original playwrights for the Tricycle Theatre of London's *The Great Game: Afghanistan*. His works have been staged throughout the United States, and in Germany, Canada, Australia, and Israel. Rogers's essays have appeared in the *New York Times*, in London's *Independent* and the *NewStatesman*, and *American Theatre*. Recent awards include Guggenheim, NEA/TCG, and NYFA fellowships; the Pinter Review Prize for Drama; the American Theatre Critics Association's Osborne New Play Award; and the William Inge Center for the Arts' New Voices Award. Rogers serves on the board of the Dramatist Guild's Dramatists Legal Defense Fund. He is an alum of New Dramatists and holds an honorary doctorate from his alma mater, the University of North Carolina School of the Arts.